cover photo : *Untitled (*female head),1982 (detail)
cover lay out : Patrick Lébedeff

editor assistant : Stéphane Argillet

*Special Thanks to :*

Alban Barré, Yannick Haennel, Élisabeth Lagane, Jean-Marc Prévost, Cathy Lenihan, Gilbert Auréjac, Birgid Schmittmann (Galerie Löhrl), Barbara Gladstone and Rainald Schumacher (Barbara Gladstone Gallery), Markus Lüttgen (Galerie Johnen & Schöttle), Bernd Klüser (Galerie Bernd Klüser)


3, RUE BEAUTREILLIS
75004 PARIS

ISBN 2-906-571-65-2

PRINTED IN EUROPE

# STEPHAN BALKENHOL

Ouvrage aidé par le Ministère français chargé de la Culture

this series edited by

*JACINTO LAGEIRA*

in the same series

JEAN-MARC BUSTAMANTE

*Christine Macel, Marc Perelman, Jacinto Lageira*

GERHARD RICHTER

*Gertrud Koch, Luc Lang, Jean-Philippe Antoine*

DAN GRAHAM

*Alain Charre, Marie-Paule Macdonald, Marc Perelman*

ROMAN OPALKA

*Christine Savinel, Jacques Roubaud, Bernard Noël*

# STEPHAN BALKENHOL

JEFF WALL

LUDGER GERDES

HERVÉ VANEL

INGRID SCHAFFNER

CONTENTS

## *An outline of a context for Stephan Balkenhol's work*

*I*t seems as if Stephan Balkenhol's sculpture has developed in a process of reaction against the orthodoxies of radical modernist plastic art. The double triumph of the aesthetic of the utterly fragmented form and its observe, the militantly unified structure, a triumph which characterizes the art of the past twenty years, creates today the situation in which a sculptor might turn toward that problematic object which is always both unified and fragmented : the human body.

In the work of Beuys above all, or of Kounellis, of Anselmo, indeed of arte povera in general, the regime of the fragmentary has been fully legitimated. This fragment, be it a shard of plaster cast, a bit sausage, or a bundle of twigs, exists as a meaningful symbol only in a context of historical and social reflection on the fate of art and its pretensions. The history of the catastrophes of our epoch, that history which arte povera recognized as having invalidated modern culture's earlier claims to universal truth, gave to its startling assemblages of objects the sense of power which comes from an act of scrupulous renunciation. This renunciation -of claims to any overarching authority in culture- was the prelude to a new experimentalism which excited the art of the 1960s and 1970s, and created the perspective of a new plastic language, open, tentative and incomplete by nature, and so filled with vistas of possibility and hope.

Coterminous with this new opening up of the forms of plastic art, the tightened and disciplined works of Judd or Andre indicated that any authentically new stage of sculptural development would have to include the negative moment of the serial, the inorganic, and the predictable, in short, of all those aspects of the built environment which created the sense of alienation so endemic to the urbanism of the 1950s and the 1960s.

The sculptural production of the period since about 1964 shows a constant dialectical movement between radically shattered and fragmented procedures and equally radically unified, condensed, and systematized ones. Often, these contradictory tendencies are visible in the work of a single artist, for example in Serra, or Ulrich Ruckriem, who was Balkenhol's teacher in Hamburg in the late 1970s.

Both major positions exclude representation as an aim of sculpture. With few exceptions, the mimetic aspects of art are replaced with the organic creation of plastic symbolic situations, as in Beuys or Kounellis, or with non-objective systematics, as with Judd. The evolution of these tendencies in fact depends on the act of exclusion of the mimetic function from sculpture and its replacement with new, experimental directions.

Along with the mimetic function, however, there disappears something very ancient and very immediate : the potential for a spontaneous form of recognition of meaning. The image of the human body remains the most directly comprehensible emblem. Across national traditions and limitations of education and language, the recognition of the attitudes, physiognomy and gestic action of the body produces a space permanently open to philosophical plastic reflection. The process of spontaneous social recognition of meaning grounds the conditions for a reception of sculpture which breaks the new bounds of the established world of art and its orthodoxies, and permits the mass of conflicting forms of cultural literacy and desire which circulate in society to impinge directly on artistic practice, or at least on reception. This interferes with the trajectory of radical modernist plastic art, which had to counterpose itself to the "popular world" of figures and figurines, in lofty or degraded forms, which always constituted the official ideology of modern public culture. The destruction of the logos of the statue has been the continuous project of modernist sculpture since Duchamp and Tatlin. However, the resulting new forms, rooted in a erudite ideology of radical openness, have begun to display their own monumental closure against the everyday world in the glamour of the triumph. In the glow of this new aura, younger artists worry that the victorious fragment has produced a universalism as dubious as the monuments it has toppled.

Moreover, the fragment, which is by nature cryptic in the sense that Walter Benjamin defined, appears to have obscured the human body of the spectator him or herself, that body whose reflection is searched for in every examination of objects.

The emphasis in the sculpture of the 1970s and 1980s on the non-bodily aspects of experience, on the experience of objects, wether fragmented or condensed, tends toward a polarized and static subject-object relationship. In this, the object, no matter how densely it is installed in a historical or semantic context, stands opposed to the body of the spectator as a theoretical thing, a thing which is at once sharply distinct from the body and which replaces it at the focal point of culture. This experience of the replacement of the body by thing is an experience of essential alienation. The creation of a cutting, illuminating experience of alienation has rightly been given a central place in the project of experimental modernist art. However, the construction of a culturally reified subject-object relationship, congealed into an exclusive concentration on objects, becomes exaggerated, one-sided and false when the spectator can no longer recognize him-or herself, as a theoretical social presence, in the world of things. During the 1980s, under conditions of a militant market-ideology in culture, the intensified glamour of the object-commodity has tended to expel the spectator from artistic space. Objects -and their representations, which are also objects- appear to populate the world of culture all on their own, and bodies, seemingly sidelined into obsolescence, can only peer into culture from a defunct exterior.

Under these conditions, the generation which has learned from arte povera and from Minimalism worries its way toward a reconsideration of the problem of the statue and its permanent functions as body-symbol and bearer of gestic meaning. Balkenhol, as a member of this generation, encounters again, from a new perspective, the problem of the statue's universalizing pretensions.

The traditional notion of the universality of meaning produced by the statue, particularly the nude, which had descended almost intact from the Greeks through to Rodin, was ruined decisively in the epoch of modernistic totalitarianism, when Fascist and Soviet art both returned to the stereotype of the noble nude in an expulsion of the challenging forms of the early avant-garde. The aggravated new monumentalism of the nude and the uniformed hero in the work of official artists in these regimes was explicitly opposed to the experimental plastic forms of Duchamp, Tatlin, Rodchenko or Picasso, forms in which the actual historical process of the fragmentation of the human being through the effects of the capitalist division of labour was made visible by means of mechanomorphic images in which human human figures are intermingled with objects. This avant-garde mechanomorphism was unacceptable to the tyrannies of the 1930s because it managed to express a sense of the catastrophic character of the modernity within which both Russia and Germany were enmeshed. The famous mechanistic figures -Duchamp's Readymades, de Chirico's Grand Metaphysician, the surrealist assemblages- provided means to perceive the shock and suffering which were produced in the elaboration of modernization, in which men, women and children were tied economically to machines at the core of the production process. This perception produced an extreme reaction against the classical ideal of statuary, whose essence was the harmonious unity of the human body. The avant-garde movements understood that industrialized modernity destroyed the social bases for such a notion of the human image, and that, under such conditions, any further promotion of the traditional ideal of statuary would be in the service of a deceptive ideology of "unity", the unity of the power state. Thus, statuary, either nude or uniformed, collapsed as a legitimate sculptural form. its place was taken by practices specifically antithetical to it, practices which investigated the spaces which were opened by the statue's disintegration as a valid emblem of the ideal state. The new practices themselves, in their programmatic openness, their refusal to establish firm boundaries between exterior and interior, sought to emblematize a different state, a more democratic, ecological one, rooted more securely in the fragile life experiences of concrete individuals.

But the utopian impact of radically open sculpture has waned. The evident capacity of the fragmented structures of 1970s plastic art to function as decorative elements in the grand museological complexes of the art world of the 1980s raises the question of how these object-clusters transcend the condition of art-commodity and retain a sense of profound meaning, however conditional. The newer "post-conceptual" object-art, which revels ironically in its commodity-status, has aggravated the kind of doubts raised by the art which preceded it. It has not created these doubts; it parasitically feeds off them, against a backdrop of social despair and complacency. The possibility of recovering the potential of the statue as an emancipatory body-symbol, one which could take up the project of experimental sculpture, not dispense with it, depends on its re-appearance as a specifically de-universalized emblem.The statue-form cannot again intervene in sculpture by simply re-assuming its function as model of a human ideal, as in classicism. Neither can Expressionism's inversion of this classicism, the idealism of exemplary suffering, provide an answer. At the same time, the nightmare history of the uniformed statue precludes a direct reinvention of the emblematic "figura" of an occupation or role in life, such as was accomplished so impressively by 19th century sculpture in the tradition of works such as Constantin Meunier's "Blacksmith". The new statue, as it might now be proposed in Balkenhol's work, is rarely nude, and it carries no attributes of occupation, labour or engagement. It develops as an incompletely particularized human figure, neither wholly shrunken into meagre individuality and solitude, nor a transcendent "Denkmodell", either classicistic or neo-expressionist. It is, strictly speaking, a monad: an isolated, condensed being, sharing some of the romantic symbolism connected to the image of the solitary tree out of which it is carved.

Balkenhol's pale monadic figures, isolated from both universality and concrete social individuation, usually appear before us simply attired, in a dress or trousers and a shirt. They are like people who have recently come out of hospital after a serious illness, who cannot yet really return to active life, but who can get dressed normally and face things again. Like convalescents, their primar occupation is to complete their recovery. Soon, they may take up their tools and re-enter their complex, stressful social relationships. The emotional world of these sculptures is arrested by their historical-aesthetic position: they are centered between a possibly volatile renunciation of the radical negations which brought the experimental forms of the 1970s into proeminence, and a thoroughgoing restoration of the idea of the socially-emblematic human figure as it really must live, work and suffer in the cities of 1988.

Balkenhol's sculptures suggest that the monadic figure may be freed from its old identity as universal abstract emblem, and so could exist not as a nostalgic residue of a past form of unity, an oppressive reminder of the 'good old days', but as a dialectical interrogation of the unachieved harmony of the existing world. Distressed by the apparent decay of open-form sculpture into cultural-décor, Balkenhol's figures attempt to stand outside open-form. His monad is thus a counter-experimental form, obliged to interrogate the language of experimental sculpture, to contemplate its peculiar silences from the viewpoint of the familiar human body. This is a body which has been erased in the stress of the struggle for the negation of oppressive, frightening statues of Colossi.

## *Balkenhol's Statues*

What makes Balkenhol's statues[1] so special? Their adamant muteness. Ordinary characters, everyday clothes, appearances, attitudes. Nothing exceptional — no unusual facial expressions, no gestures or poses.

Not that the figures are fully expressionless or meaningless for that matter. However calm the human body and face may appear, they can never be fully expressionless, at least exhibiting restraint, inwardness, calm or contemplation. Balkenhol's figures show scarcely anything more than these basics of the expressible. Joy, sadness, agitation, tension and so on are only faintly hinted at, barely visible below the surface.

In the same way, the statues reveal no deep meanings. But yet they're not meaningless. Clothing, limbs, full figures are represented.

[1] Translator's note: the German for 'statue' is *Standbild*, literally 'standing picture'. While English would be hard-pressed to refer to a sculpture as a picture (*Bild*), it is quite natural to do so in German; indeed this literal usage is central to the author's argument.

Above and beyond their basic objectiveness, they neither embody nor proffer any further meaning: they don't stand for any determinate human type, or social class, cannot be identified as representing any particular person, nor do they have any allegorical or symbolic function.

To many viewers, their poverty of expression and meaning makes them seem boring, bland and without interest. When somebody goes to the trouble of carving an almost life-size figure — so the reasoning goes — he must want to communicate something. This expectation is thwarted. An expectation that other sculptors still (or once again) working in the figurative tradition are only too happy to fulfill with gusto, giving vent to a strong neo-expressionism. Balkenhol renews with the use of figurative images, though not of course in the old established way: he neither pulls pseudo-archaic ingredients out of the pressure cooker in the myth-making style of Lüpertz, nor does he go for John Ahearn style socio-empirical case studies, let alone certain forms of ghost-train expressionism typical of some recent German sculpture.

Balkenhol doesn't offer us a morsel of determinate meaning, no finished image for us to get used to, store away and pack around in our memory. The figures tell no story, refer to nothing, have no message to convey — there is simply nothing special whatsoever about them. But it is precisely this which makes them exceptional. The power of the imagination is not neutralized but is instead

immediately stimulated by the statues' mute reserve. The powers of representation kick in because at the moment of perception there is no given content whatsoever. The power of the imagination is quickened instead of being placated by some outside idea.

Balkenhol's figures hint at what constitutes the image of man as it appears to us. They are neither based on or cast from specific individuals, nor are they carefully crafted copies of human forms. They hint at the human body, but these hints are brought out in raw wood, left unplaned, unsmoothed, unfinished. The grooves of the chisel are still seen in the wood's surface, traces of its honing in on form. These traces stand for the approach of human perception to form: just as the gaze puts form together piece by piece, after having first seen it as a whole possessing its own shape, just as one comes to learn the particularities of a body by running one's fingertips over it, in showing the gouges and hesitations of the chisel in the wood, these works are a means of approaching the figure. Because the individual steps in the sculptural process can be seen in the work, they can be compared with the very process of seeing; they are comparable in terms of scope and precision to what is customarily perceived by the senses of sight and touch. These works provide an occasion to reflect on the status and limits of one's own powers of perception. One sees arms or a head as a figurative whole, but one also sees traces left by the tools in the wood as they created the arms or the face; a specific whole brought out through a series of separate actions. In this way, these statues are pictures of an approach to people.

This is less trivial than it may appear. It is significant and exceedingly important. More and more, our visual culture is losing touch with the basic work of keen perception. Photographic visualizing encourages looking at the whole, at the expense of looking with precision and in detail. Precise looking is documented in drawings, where it is in its natural environment. When a person draws an object naturalistically, he is forced to close in upon the object's qualities right up to the limits of his vision. This results in a highly differentiated and subtle way of handling reality. One can study for instance the resulting profundity and exhaustiveness of this way of looking in the drawings of the nineteenth century. Photographic visualizing tends to make approaching the object in such a discerning way superfluous. As a result, a person now "knows" pictures of the most divergent and remote things in the world, but is unable to see, imagine or describe these things with any exactitude. The quantity of pictures grows ever larger, and yet ever less precise. While photography is apparently increasing our volume of knowledge, it is at the same time undermining the very roots of our ability to know[2].

Balkenhol's statues (*Standbilder*) form alternatives to the status of pictures (*Stand der Bilder*).

[2] This can be seen in drawings themselves. Compare drawings by architects in the nineteenth century with drawings by today's postmodern architects, for whom drawing once again plays an important role. In comparison to the earlier architects' drawings, the latter frequently look like childish attempts. That alone wouldn't be too serious if it didn't document a banal fact of seeing which, in the buildings that are erected from the drawings, sadly becomes crude reality. The state of visual culture is therefore almost a political issue.

Although Balkenhol's works testify to a sensual, sensitive approach to an object, he does not work "at gut level", to employ the self-actualizationists' somewhat unappetizing expression. He has not fallen victim to the fatal belief that only by giving expression to one's innermost experience, to one's most authentic feelings can art be guaranteed as acceptable. He sets himself apart from the vulgar expressionist whose intimate self-experience is always the source and object of his art, whose production is a mere effusion of sensitivity, compensating for such narcissistic isolation only by fostering a cult around the myth of his inspired creative powers. Balkenhol doesn't bash the raw material in order to express his sensitivity or to soundly influence the viewer. He forgoes tasteful betting on crude and robust strokes, eschewing spontaneity and intuition as fake symbols of freedom and creativity.

What Balkenhol does provide are pictures of a communicative approach to objects, of a dialogue with them. He doesn't just take something and willfully form or deform it heeding only his subjective intentions and feelings. He doesn't lead us on with the illusion of the foot-loose and fancy-free art hero, the illusion of the unbridled creator who feels no restraint beyond his own ego. With short, energetic though non-aggressive strokes of the chisel, he shapes protrusions and hollows, recesses and swellings, muscles, limbs, and bodies. He respects the natural human figure, attempting it would seem to approach it by means of touch, obtaining figurativeness by accepting its individual peculiarities. His is an art which is more than a mere copy (*Nach-Stellen*) of reality, involving instead the mental conception (*Vor-Stellen*) of images and pictures, with which people can begin to grasp reality. Because these works both exemplify and symbolize an attentive, respectful approach to nature, Balkenhol avoids its subjugation to the "free" subjective phantasmagoria of the ego. He proceeds cautiously, symbolizing perhaps humility — a subdued, restrained existence. It is because Balkenhol's statues are related to conventional sculpture that they are original and distinct from it: his figures neither stride energetically forth, nor are they despairing, downtrodden victims. They stand before us, reserved, silent, watching.

Balkenhol's statues are like a symbolic embodiment of the addressee standing facing us, of a partner in dialogue. To contemplate these figures is always like the standing in front of someone. They refer to the stance and position of people in regard to the world. Yet, narration plays virtually no part in Balkenhol's art. He employs minimal forms of expression, his pictures are human — but they are not pictures of human beings. Balkenhol questions the role in art of human beings and their images, as if to suggest how these roles ought to be filled.

The figures are in no sense illusionistic. They rely neither on optical illusion nor on fraudulent content: they are ways of closing in on human likeness, but are free from connotations of an ideal, a hero, an archetype, a man thrown into the world, a man in the street, etc. Just as these pictures are not expressionistic, they also

have nothing to do with Pop Art, which ascribes no intrinsic value to the image itself, subordinating it to the medium, a message, or some trivial extrinsic purpose. They are clearly not duplicates of already existing pictures or ways of seeing, as Pop Art images are, and which are for that very reason so disappointing.

Balkenhol's works strike me as being essentially hints or indications: just as they never show a completely "exact" representation of the body's form, they never provide exact answers to the question to which they constantly allude: the role of objective, figurative sculpture. Balkenhol sets out a line of inquiry, aiming at a blind spot in the predominant abstract sculpture of this century. He points to all the unanswered questions: questions about a subtler, more differentiated figurativeness than that of Pop and Neo-expressionism; questions about the meaning of anthropomorphism in an industrialized world; the question of human scale; the question of mimesis which art felt it had gone beyond and forgotten. He questions the role of craftsmanship, and the visual rhetoric of pictures and sculptures, questioning their role in the human world-identifying and world-shaping process. And he questions the role of the monument and its use in the dignifying of human living space with pictures and sculptures of people. Not that Balkenhol withholds all the answers. Perhaps he gives the answer by leaving the questions open. And that is what's so wonderful about his statues: you never know what they're staring at, you don't know where they're looking. They produce such suspense because one always has the feeling there is something which still remains to be said. They are so refreshingly "empty" as opposed to other message-laden pictures. Pictures which testify to nothing but themselves and to the power of pictures.

Balkenhol, who studied at the Hamburg Academy with Ülrich Rückriem, comes out of the tradition of abstract sculpture. Like many other young artists of his generation, he could see no further sense in the pursuit of purely abstract, predominantly minimalistic work. Continuing on from the existing positions, only repetition, hairsplitting, and atomization were conceivable. In the place of formalism and abstraction, figurative work, that many thought had disappeared from art forever, once again began to look like an interesting option.

Balkenhol did not follow the decreed "hunger for pictures[3]", the feeding of the "starving (upper) class" with some sort of picture potpourri or a handed-down stock of picture conserves. His work is an attempt at closing in on the pictorial in sculpture, an investigation of the conditions and possibilities of figurative representation. In this respect his work still stands in the tradition of work by sculptors like Rückriem — if they are properly understood — as a sort of investigation into the groundwork and primary elements of sculpture and plasticity. So just as Balkenhol's undisguised chisel marks can be seen in the tradition of Rückiem's signs of the elementary sculptural process, so can Balkenhol's way

[3] The author is referring to the book by Wolfgang Max Faust and Gerd de Vries, *Hunger nach Bildern - Deutsche Malerei der Gegenwart*, published in 1982 and known for its vehement defence of German neo-expressionist painting.

of installing his work be seen in the tradition of his teacher. When Balkenhol installs his own work, he does it in direct response to the characteristics and proportions of the space where it is to be installed. (Practically all sculptors make this same claim for themselves — but what counts of course are not the good intentions but the results, and these are only seldom so successful as Balkenhol's.) Balkenhol has developed an unusual plinth for his statues: a combination of a pedestal and a console. This type of mount makes explicit reference to architecture, the device explicitly associating the figure standing upon it with the wall that it is standing against. The works are often presented either implicitly or explicitly as reliefs and accentuate thereby the shift from up flatness to space, to use a notion of Adolf von Hildebrand. The works are always integrated into their architectural environment and also hint at taking a step into this space. Scarcely any other young sculptor has developed and mastered such clear links to architecture as Balkenhol.

Just as the works stimulate the imaginative power of the viewer precisely because they say virtually nothing, they also refer to the room through the way they occupy its space, without completely taking it over. In otherwise entirely commonplace exhibition spaces, Balkenhol's figures unmistakably activate the place where they are standing. Up against these figures, one feels enclosed by the system of axes and associations the figures' austere installation brings into play. These works don't function as pictures placed haphazardly in a room, whose only purpose is that they be perceived there. They always confer a distinct stamp upon the room they are in.

In most cases, exhibition spaces are otherwise indistinct — one interchangeable with another. As rooms, such spaces are as neutral as possible so as to not distract from the works exhibited in them; normally, autonomous works establish no connection with the space they're in. Balkenhol on the other hand brings the indistinct, speechless, meaningless room into the picture, making it into a life-size model, a room specifically shaped by sculpture. Internally, Balkenhol's sculptures, through tangible actions on the raw material, always make the transformation to a figurative form of representation visible. Externally, they make vividly graphic the shift from an insignificant place to a contoured, unmistakably unique location.

Balkenhol's works evoke human themes, and their installation evokes the theme of the shaping of human space, through likenesses of people. These are tricky themes. And the value of Balkenhol's art lies in the fact that it doesn't shy away from them, yet suggests no answers, for the questions remain open. His is an art that leaves something imaginable which cannot yet be felt: the reserved, peacefully contemplative presence of people in space.

## *Dummies*

> Dummy: *n., pl. -mies 1. A person unable to talk; mute: an obsolescent term; 2. a figure made in human form, as for displaying clothing, practising tackling in football, etc.; 3. an imitation or sham; substitute for real thing, as an empty container or false drawer; 4. a person secretly acting for another while apparently representing his or her interests; 5. [Slang] a stupid person [...]*[1].

Certain artists find themselves obliged — by critics or by their own reticence to theorize their artistic practice — to define not what they do but rather what they do not do. This is in part what Stephan Balkenhol does when he defines his work: "My sculptures are relatively realistic, [which] means they can all be recognized right away. They've got particular facial features and postures, yet they don't depict anyone in particular. They are not meant to tell a story either — they are not meant to have a narrative function[2]." This

[1] *Webster's New World Dictionary*, New York: Simon & Schuster, 1994.

[2] Quoted by Neal Benezra, "Refiguring a Tradition", *Stephan Balkenhol*, Hirschhorn Museum and Sculpture Garden, Smithsonian Institute, Washington D.C., 19 October/15 January 1995, p. 28. (Henceforth: Washington 1995.)

exclusion of all the traditional functions of representation, liable to survive parasitically in an almost abstract perception of the figure recalls, notably, postwar developments in "expressionist"-type figurative representation. Bacon, Giacometti, or more recently Baselitz whose upside-down figures almost efface themselves in their pirouette, similarly refuse to allow figurative representation to become frozen in illustration or description. For a German artist born in 1957 like Balkenhol, Baselitz no doubt incarnates the generation toward which he has to position himself. The violence and the disquieting fusion between representation and its object, characteristic of certain neo-expressionist works, are clearly foreign to Balkenhol's work, as is the conservatism of a figurative sculptor like Robert Graham whose *Lises* series in the seventies — a small, super-detailed, feminine figure in bronze, set on a conspicuous plinth — may be thought of as the rear guard of what Edward Lucie-Smith calls "super-realist" sculpture[3]. Yet Balkenhol's sculpture discards nothing of these two antinomical aesthetics out of hand; instead he refuses to choose between them. His method is apparently based on stirring up the very conventions on which it relies, regaining classical coherency just when it seems to be negating it, and vice versa.

This complex attitude is probably rooted in his years of study with Ülrich Rückriem with whom he was both student and studio

[3] Edward Lucie-Smith, *Sculpture since 1945*, Oxford: Phaidon Press, 1987, pp. 59-71, and the exhibition catalogue *Robert Graham Statues*, Walker Art Center, Minneapolis, Sept. 13/Nov. 8, 1981.

assistant. Which is another way of saying that toward the end of the seventies, he was in close contact with an artist whose monumental stone work suppresses its profoundly figurative connections beneath its "minimalist" exterior. "The history of Ülrich Rückriem", observes Laszlo Gloser, "can be deciphered like an archeological dig: the abstract and avant-garde stone works are the most apparent level — but watch out: he is an artist who at the same time does commissioned portraits of striking resemblance[4]." For student and assistant, this separation between two modes of production (each one appearing as the disgrace of the other) could only reinforce the feeling of a "taboo" against representation of the human figure[5], that ran through the 70's. Balkenhol, referring to his own and Rückriem's work as "opposite ends of the same thing[6]", is no doubt aware of this suppression of the figure in Rückriem's work and, in some way, avenges it. At the beginning of the eighties, he visited the major

[4] See Laszlo Gloser, "Les chemins qui mènent au monument", *Ülrich Rückriem, Sculptures*, Centre Georges Pompidou, Musée National d'Art Moderne, 16 March - 9 May 1983, pp. 69-75.

[5] The situation does however seem more complex than Laszlo Gloser might lead us to suppose. In a discussion with Balkenhol, Rückriem claimed he was too "cowardly" to do portraits, mentioning that in the past he had done them for alimentary reasons (no doubt in the genre of the 1964 sculpture shown in Gloser's text), and adding that he would not be adverse to doing some in the future. See "Excerpt by Ülrich Rückriem from a Conversation between Ülrich Rückriem and Stephan Balkenhol on October 27, 1992", cat. *Stephan Balkenhol About Men and Sculpture*, Witte de With Center for Contemporary Art, December 12, 1992/January 24, 1993, supplement, p. 3.

[6] Stephan Balkenhol, *Possible Worlds, Sculpture from Europe*, Institute of Contemporary Arts, Serpentine Gallery, London, November 6, 1990/January 6, 1991 (interview with Iwona Blazwick, James Lingwood and Andrea Schlieker, London, 21 September 1990), p. 27. Balkenhol himself mentions the importance of the figure in Rückriem's work in his conversation with Philippe Vergne, "Stephan Balkenhol, De l'autre côté du miroir", *Parachute*, n°. 72, October-November-December 1993, p. 25.

European museums, studied figurative public (ie. monumental) sculpture, made drawings from roman busts and Greek Kouroi, and took photos which are still hanging next to the drawings pinned to his studio wall. It may have been this educational tour which led him to the conclusion that he had to “reinvent the figure”, arguing “the tradition had been interrupted[7]”. But at the same time, without any apparent contradiction, he has situated his work beyond the debates around modernism and the desire to “reactivate” tradition[8]. In fact, moving away from his experiment in casting objects in frozen fabric, the inevitable thawing and collapse of which was an ironic comment on the hyper-realist sculptures of John de Andrea or Duane Hanson, he returned to carving wood sculptures of human heads as he had done in his youth, after numerous visits to the “Realism” Pavilion at Documenta 5 in 1972 incited him to make his “own Pop art[9].”

[7] Stephan Balkenhol, “Conversation between Stephan Balkenhol and Thomas Schütte, September 1992”, in *About Men and Sculpture*, op. cit., p. 12.

[8] Conversation with Philippe Vergne, *Parachute*, op. cit., p.25. This approach to art history, neither wishing to carry on a tradition nor eliminating it from his work, can be seen in the way he sculpts. More than anything, it was market forces which, by quickly grabbing up Balkenhol's work, allowed him to escape from a process of strict repetition (and the anguish that goes with it), enabling him to work on each sculpture in independence, because he was rid of thephysical presence of his eaarlier works, whose latent presence was nevetheless preserved by the documents pinned to the wall.

[9] “Balkenhol recalls having been fundamentally influenced by the figurative work he saw at ‘Documenta 5’, when he determined to ‘make my own Pop art.’” Neal Benezra, Washington 1995, p. 24. The American “Photo-Realists”, well represented at Kassel in 1972, thought of their own work as within the Pop-art tradition. See “The Photo-Realists: 12 Interviews…” and “The Verist Sculptures: 2 Interviews”, *Art in America*, vol. 60, n°. 6, November-December 1972, pp. 73-99. Elsewhere, Balkenhol has admitted that he began by doing Pop art and assemblages, before other influences led him on to other things. See *Possible Worlds*, op. cit., p. 27.

For the past fifteen or so years, Balkenhol has been producing figurative sculpture in which the painted wood's appearance always shows a somewhat rough finish. We find four basic types of representations: the generic figure of (western) men and women; animal sculpture; men/animals in association; and hybrids of the two. Apparently only the human figure is used in high relief and bas-relief, sometimes ambiguously entitled *Relief Paintings*[10]. Although his work was at first frozen in the recognition of a fixed and indifferent archetype, certain more recent works, *Large Classical Man* (1996) and *Large Relief Painting (Yellow)* (1996), may contradict such an approach, though without completely refuting it. The 1985 work, *Three Figures*, remains a striking example of the recognition of this stereotype despite variations in posture and in the color of otherwise identical clothing. Clearly not showing specific individuals undergoing some ordeal, the objective is rather to save the appearances of an endangered species — the human species and above all an artistic species: figurative representation. To a very high degree (same postures, same colors more or less), Balkenhol replaced the human faces in *Three Figures* with the heads of a cow, a lion and a bird of prey. The after-effects of the graft are invisible: there is nothing monstrous in the result, and the animal, frozen in position, is perfectly humanized, docile and standardized.

It is not only his recourse — some would say return — to the figure which sets Balkenhol apart from the abstract sculpture of

[10] *Screen (Man and Ant)* (1996) is an exception.

the sixties, but also, his way of conceiving space. Well-known as they are, Tony Smith's answers to the questions raised by his 183cm-sided *Die* are nonetheless explicit:

> Q. Why didn't you make it larger so that it would loom over the observer?
> A. I was not making a monument.
> Q. Then why didn't you make it smaller, so that the observer could see over the top?
> A. I was not making an object[11].

Smith's conception of space is profoundly non-hierarchical. It supposes, as Robert Morris points out, that the spectator become aware that he too occupies the same space as the work whose *presence* must neither dominate nor be restricted[12]. On the contrary, whether Balkenhol's statues are monumental miniaturized, or just slightly bigger or smaller than human size, the sculptor insists on a clear separation of spaces. "It's necessary to differentiate between human-size and sculpture-size, to clearly map out an imaginative space. People should never think when they see a sculpture: 'There's a standing man...' [...] The important thing for me is not so much what position they have, as long as the position appears natural and self-evident[13]." In short, Balkenhol refuses to allow us to perceive his sculpture as a "substitute for a person — in other words as a kind of *statue*", as Michael Fried pejoratively

[11] Quoted by Robert Morris in the epigraph to his "Notes on Sculpture", Part II, in Gregory Battock (ed.), *Minimal Art A Critical Perspective,* New York: E. P. Dutton, 1968, pp. 228-230.
[12] Ibid.
[13] Stephan Balkenhol, *Possible Worlds*, op. cit., p. 28.

deduced from what Smith said about his Die[14]. Indeed for Balkenhol, “making a human-size sculpture gives only reduced pleasure[15].” As if to ward off any “latent or hidden naturalism” (to employ the terms Fried applied to Smith), the natural appears for Balkenhol to be profoundly cultural. The disappearance of the nude in the 1980's and the “clothing” of his sculpted figures was in fact justified by a strange respect for social conventions. “As you normally don't encounter people in the nude”, explains Balkenhol simply, “I dress my figures in ordinary, everyday clothes[16].” Conforming to a moral order condemning any transgression, his sculptures are nevertheless separated from the spectator's space by a plinth made from the same block of wood as the sculptures themselves[17]. But Balkenhol's insistence on distance and his sculpture's “objectiveness” remains tightly bound up with a contrasting factor: “a sometimes very violent, even bothersome presence in keeping with a classical conception of sculpture[18].” So in 1993, when

[14] Michael Fried, “Art and Objecthood”, *Artforum*, June 1967, reprinted in Gregory Battock (ed.), *Minimal Art*, op. cit., pp. 116-147

[15] Stephan Balkenhol, “Interview” (June 1994), by Alexandra Midal, in Cat. *Stephan Balkenhol*, Musée départemental de Rochechouart, July 8/September 18, 1994, p. 11. (Henceforth: Rochechouart, 1994.)

[16] Stephan Balkenhol, *Possible Worlds*, op. cit., p. 28.

[17] “I use the plinth to create a certain distance, to establish a relation between the volume and the space. [...] [The plinth itself] always remains subordinated to the sculpture standing on it. More than the plinth, it's the volume which is essential to me.” Stephan Balkenhol, Rochechouart 1994, p. 11. And on another occasion: “in the same way, to avoid outside elements getting added to my sculptures, I make the plinths myself and integrate them into the sculpture [...]. In this way, I'm sure that the sculpture is always shown properly, that there's no mistake.” Conversation with Philippe Vergne, *Parachute*, op. cit., p.24.

[18] Stephan Balkenhol, Rochechouart 1994, pp.8 and 12.

Balkenhol showed *Three Big Naked Women* in Cologne, one critic was particularly sensitive to "the life of these wooden beings, and their desire to live among us in the real physical world rather than as abstract, material art objects[19]."

This presence, generally speaking, cannot stem from such an empathetic relation to his figures. Rather it is brought about by the confusion of scale and the number of sculptures which, sometimes, make up a single work. His 1992 work, *Ten Column Sculptures*, looks like a display of the diversity of his work, and could at the same time be seen as a collection of rough-hews for monumental works. In it we see two animals — a fish and a cat— a full-size figure of an ordinary man, an ordinary woman naked, an ordinary woman dressed in a light blue dress sitting on a circus stool, the crowned (and proportionately monumental) head of the ordinary man, etc. The man/animal combination and the hybrids are only hinted at by the figure of a man on all fours. Two figurines, one combining the head of the standard man with a spherical body, the other showing the full-sized man standing on the globe of the Earth, strangely echo one another. The former reduces the latter's power to the laughable image of a plaything that, whichever way you push it, always springs back to its initial position of equilibrium. Accordingly, the apparent inertia of Balkenhol's sculpture remains unperturbed by this playful side. At any rate, once the shock (or the humor) of the scale has worn off, the sculpture assumes a more

[19] Norbert Messler, "Stephan Balkenhol", *Artforum*, vol. XXXII, n°. 4, December 1993, p.92.

tempered look — as far from the glacial gaze of 70's hyper-realist sculpture ("nothing is more dead than a cast of the living body[20]") as from expressionist effusion. These normalized figures whose composure, clothing, and distant expression (or relative absence thereof) are part and parcel of a perfectly integrated social code, make their way between embarrassing presence and relative discretion — all of which makes for a pretty uncomfortable situation.. The only really physical solicitation comes from the works' invariably "unfinished" character, clearly foreign — in its very constancy and regularity —to any drama whatsoever. The eye may even accord itself the pleasure of smoothing over the somewhat rough texture, thereby giving a polish to a gesture which in its very lack of finish, discretely preserves the traces of the sculptor's know-how[21]. No expressionism actually shows through the surface, and the gesture's presence attests more to the sculptor's mastery than to some creative urgency or fit of anger he felt, which might be to the viewer's detriment. Nor are his figures affected by the unevenness of the texture. This sort of distinction between the figure's presence and the autonomy of the material in which it has been carved shows up when for instance there is a visible split or knot in the wood. If Balkenhol is concerned with these accidents which are part of a sculpture's life, he clearly "doesn't make use of them[22]."

[20] Stephan Balkenhol, "The Body is the Present", *Witte de With, The Lectures*, Witte de With Center for Contemporary Art, Rotterdam, 1993, p. 92.
[21] "The marks left by the chisel are not intended to show my work process", Balkenhol insists, rejecting, in the obviousness of the gesture, anything to do with expressionist pathos. See *Possible Worlds*, op. cit., p.27.
[22] See Rochechouart 1994, p. 8.

The wood and the unconcealed chisel strokes imply however a physical and sensual relation to the material, that Balkenhol insists upon. "There's a distinction between a sculptor who cuts stone or wood and a sculptor who molds plaster or clay," he explains, "between a sculptor who uses a hard material that in itself has volume, and a sculptor who creates works from the inside out, by modeling. I'm a sculptor in the sense of going into the material. I like the different states of matter. Right from the outset, the form of the wood seems to contain the sculpture [...]. Yes, the material imposes a dialogue, a form of resistance which dictates how fast the work will be done[23]." It may be pointed out that if Balkenhol seems to use primarily a variety of softwoods such as wawa, he also uses other woods, whose nature can influence the outcome of the work. In any case, the distance he establishes with the wood's natural physiognomy differs sharply from the organic relationship characteristic of early expressionism. A 1912 drawing by Ernst Ludwig Kirchner, for example, shows a figure drawn inside a contorted trunk whose twists affect the way the body bends. Conversely, a drawing by Balkenhol, actually entitled *Where to Put the Arms,* seems to show the insertion of several figures into a parallelepiped that has been divided into four vertical rectangles, evoking a block of wood which has already been squared up for use[24].

[23] Conversation with Philippe Vergne, *Parachute*, op. cit., p. 25.

[24] See ill. 4, in the article by Wolfgang Henze, "Genèse de la sculpture expressioniste", *Figure du moderne, l'expressionisme en Allemagne*, Musée d"Art Moderne de la Ville de Paris, November 18, 1992/March 14, 1993, p.71. On Balkenhol's drawings, see Washington 1995, fig. 9, p. 29. This sort of drawing also recalls the articulated structure of the screens Balkenhol did. Some of his works, such as the female part of his 1995 *Relief Volume I and II (Male and Female)* (cat. 31, Washington 1995) or *Through the Trees*, 1995, corroborate this manner of setting the body in volume, suggested by the drawing.

In this case, it is indeed "its block appearance which gives the sculpture its monoxylousness, [which] confers a density and unity[25]." The very mass from which his figures emerge imposes a correction on the material's anomalies, negating its natural origin, just as Balkenhol's figures (including his animal figures) always appear perfectly sociable. Stated differently, Balkenhol's figurative sculpture generally upholds an ultra-classic rigor: "simplicity in the choice of subject, simplicity of expression, simplicity in the forms, in the attitudes: such is the first rule that the sculptor has to observe if he is to produce works of beauty, and even in order to not produce ridiculous ones[26]." In 1981, his drawing of the sculpted Laocoon group showed the ironic distance that Balkenhol established with such doctrine, in that it was a caricature of "The" model for moderating the passions, in the aesthetics of neoclassicism[27]. The gesticulating of the characters is at once grotesque and stiff, and Laocoon's pain is apparently the result of an inadvertent pencil stroke in drawing the snake which is moving in to injure his eye. To some

[25] Stephan Balkenhol, Rochechouart 1994, pp. 10-11.

[26] François Gizot, *Essai sur les limites qui séparent et les liens qui unissent les Beaux-Arts*, 1816-1818, La Rochelle: Rumeurs des Ages, Coll. Passage/Parole, 1995, p. 31.

[27] "The calmer the body's attitude, the more apt it is to express the true character of the soul: in all those positions which move too far from a restful position, the soul is no longer in its most natural state, it finds itself in a state of violence and constraint. It is in such states of violent passion that it recognizes itself most easily but, on the other hand, it is great and noble in the state of rest and harmony. For the Laocoon, pain shown by itself would have been *parenthyrsis*. It is for this reason that the artist, in order to unify the soul's character and nobility, gave Laocoon the attitude which, even in such throws of pain, was closest to restfulness." Johan J. Winckelmann, *Réflexions sur l'imitation des oeuvres grecques en peinture et en sculpture* (1775), Nimes: Ed. Jacqueline Chambon, 1991, p. 36. Balkenhol's untitled drawing is reproduced in Washington 1995, ill. 7, p. 27.

extent, the man/animal associations (lion, giraffe, bull, crocodile...), as crazy as they are, and without any of the drama such confrontations might imply, suggest the same irony. In spite of establishing this ironic distance, and his penchant for strange imaginings, Balkenhol nonetheless advocates a perfectly classical restraint: "I'm not looking for an expressive acme", he states clearly, "a man who is crying or laughing is petrified in his expression[28]."

Without entirely excluding from his sculpture the tendency toward caricature, expressed most notably in his drawings, that thereby preserve an ironic distance with his subject, a certain discomfort ends up troubling our exaggeratedly tranquil perception of his specimen of western man. The latter indeed corresponds less to an ideal than to an average genre which we would be hard pressed to take as a model. This lack of exaltation may appear, as Paul Ardenne has noted, to be a clue (by default) to a critical dimension: "The primacy of the radiant body, insisted on by humanism, is abolished by the figure's presence which, though of course undeniable, is essentially cold, able at once to attract our gaze and to hold it at a distance." However, taken in by the "paradoxical beauty, as serene as it is unsettling" of a sculpture "fortified by its profound homogeneity, by its high quotient of universality[29]," the praise can also be enlisted — as we shall see — by the negative

[28] Stephan Balkenhol, Rochechouart 1994, p. 6.

[29] See the critique by Paul Ardenne, "Stephan Balkenhol", *Art Press*, n°. 175, December 1992, p. 76. Paul Ardenne had nevertheless sensed the limits of this seduction when he judged the Thames exhibition of Balkenhol's *Standing Figure on Buoy* to be "improper".

critique of Balkenhol's sculpture. The perplexity which his figures engender is guaranteed only within the space of an artistic institution (gallery or museum). Given the proximity to the work, and the "specialized" public that gallery space supposes, the way of looking differs from that of the most "general" public which Balkenhol also wishes to address when he exposes his sculpture in an open space.

So Balkenhol sculpts "just to see if it is possible to end up renewing a tradition from which [he is] at the same time liberating [himself][30]." This style of play doesn't go over well with other artists of his generation. Above and beyond his work's lack of intellectual content, Thomas Schütte has accused Balkenhol of carrying on a bad joke[31]. This criticism, in a backhanded kind of way, touches on the Pop art aspect of Balkenhol's sculpture. In the 1960's, Harold Rosenberg — returning the negative critique of Pop art as "an art which is too easily assimilated [...] which requires neither sensitivity nor intellectual effort[32]" — saw the "narcotic reiteration" of Warhol's Campbell's Soup labels "like a joke without humor told over and over again, until it carried a hint of menace[33]..." When Balkenhol

[30] Conversation with Philippe Vergne, Parachute, op. cit., p.24. He mentions, amongst other, his *Rider* (1986) for Jenisch Park-Skulptur in Hamburg.

[31] "Let me put it in harsh words: these figures are somewhat like the joke, "A man went to see the doctor..." when everybody starts laughing even before the digressions tell them what the problem is. [...] My criticism - I don't know if it's really criticism, yet - is that they are so void, your figures." Thomas Schütte to Stephan Balkenhol, in *About Men and Sculpture*, op. cit., p.13.

[32] Peter Selz, "Pop go the Artists", *Partisan Review* 30, n°.3, Summer 1963, p.316. See also "A Symposium on Pop Art", *Arts* 37, n°.7, April 1963, pp.36-44.

[33] Harold Rosenberg, "The Game of Illusion: Pop and Gag", *The Anxious Object, Art Today and Its Audience*, New York: Horizon Press, 1964, p.75.

repeats the same figure, he nevertheless plays with variations in postures and the color of clothes (*Relief* 1983, and *Three Figures* 1985, cat. 1 & 5, Washington 1995) to get away from the anesthesia linked to the repetition of the identical. However, in the long term, these marks of superficial distinctions underscore the figures' equivalence more than their difference. The only effect of introducing variation in this way was to defer the discomfort, perhaps in order to increase it, that comes from recognizing the stereotype on which figurative representation is founded. Balkenhol may be offering a sort of television image which keeps repeating the same program while changing ever so slightly the details — which, for Warhol, was what characterized television's inadequacy. Carefully avoiding the logic of repetition pushed right to the limit — as Warhol did —, only leading to repeating *exactly* the same thing, Balkenhol does not exhaust its value as a show, and finds himself accused of tending dangerously toward the facile. For some, the modulating of repetition in Balkenhol's work is part of a procedure which recalls certain aspects of Pop art, but without the critical connotations[34]. His detractors suspect him in this sense of bringing back a reactionary ideology and a conservative force, hostile to the autonomy of art, in a "figurative work [which] very often tends not to provoke, not to stimulate thoughts, because it uses a certain set of signs. And people

[34] As pointed out by Kathleen Goggin, "Stephan Balkenhol", *Parachute*, n°.83, July-August-September, 1996, pp. 44-45. Two of Balkenhol's drawings, reproduced in the preamble to the catalogue (Washington 1995), show pediments of religious buildings decorated with pictures of a stylized Mickey Mouse. Above and beyond the irony of using this motif, it possibly recalls Claes Oldenburg's *Mouse Museum* - which just happened to have been shown at Documenta 5 in 1972.

are used to reading these signs[35]…." It is perhaps the distinctive feature of Balkenhol's work to awake such suspicion, and the artist purposefully fosters this tension[36].

This lack of critical thrust might be thought to connect Balkenhol's sculpture, certain reliefs of which have been described as "polaroids in wood", to a sort of "Post 'Post Pop Art'", to use and extend a term which in the seventies designated the artists of American photo-realism[37]. It could be in fact that their strong showing at Documenta 5 is not unrelated to the uncommitted appearance which today seems to ratify a "generic" definition of the human figure in Balkenhol's work[38]. The absence of any socio-political discourse that many photo-realists insist upon, already flew in the face of what was expected of such realism[39]. A similar contradiction also motivates Balkenhol's paradoxical vision of a return to the figurative tradition as a means for human beings to "reproduce images of their inexistence[40]." Gerhard Richter for instance, when asked what motivated his choice of subjects, replied that it was a "choice by elimination". He claimed he

35 Ludger Gerdes, in "The Body is the Present", in *Witte de With, The Lectures*, op. cit., p. 97.
36 "A lot of people think they understand the work I do they think that it is nice and wonderful because they can see that it is handmade and not abstract. I don't want to change my art because there are some people who understand it." Ibid, p. 94.
37 "What interests me particularly about the relief is the trompe l'oeil effect: you pretend there is more volume and plasticity than there really is." Stephan Balkenhol, *Possible Worlds*, op. cit., p. 28.
38 To use a term Balkenhol employed in his conversation with Philippe Vergne, *Parachute*, op. cit., p. 25.
39 According to Lawrence Alloway ("'Reality': Ideology at D5", *Artforum*, vol. 11, no. 2, October 1972, p. 31), one of the (unfulfilled) objectives of Documenta 5 was to confront photo-realism with Soviet style socialist realism, thus setting communist and capitalist ideologies back to back.
40 Stephan Balkenhol, Rochechouart 1994, p. 14

"tried to eliminate everything which touched on known problems or issues, whether they be pictorial, social, or aesthetic. I try to find nothing too explicit, hence all these banal subjects; and then, afterwards, I try to avoid allowing the banal to become my problem and my trademark. It is a totally evasive action, in a way[41]." In the United States in 1972, Robert Bechtle set down the following approach, fairly representative of the concerns of many hyper-realists: "I do relate to those things I paint — suburban houses, cars, relatives. Yet on the other hand I try to preserve a kind of neutrality which doesn't tell the viewer what to think about all this. I'm not making a social comment about the middle class; I'm not saying that what I picture is good or bad. It's up to the viewer to make up his own response[42]." Basically, Balkenhol doesn't stray far from this idea when making "a realistic figure which generates abstract feelings in the spectator[43]."

Moreover, like photo-realism in the 1970's, Balkenhol's art may be thought of as a manifesto for bringing back a broken tradition. A critical interpretation of this kind, tacitly based on the domination (and institutionalization) of abstraction[44], imagines this "bringing

[41] Interview with Rolf Günter Dienst, 1970, in Hans-Ulrich Obrist (ed.), *The Daily Practice of Painting, Writings and Interviews*, London: Thames and Hudson, 1995, p. 62.

[42] Linda Chase, Nancy Foote, Ted McBurnett, "The Photo-Realists: 12 Interviews", *Art in America*, vol. 60, no. 6, November - December 1972, p. 74. Tom Blackwell (p. 76), like many others, recognized his debt to Pop art, but stressed one difference: "Pop art was deliberately trying to make a kind of ironic statement about American culture and about the vulgarization of the world...."

[43] Stephan Balkenhol, *Possible Worlds, op. cit.*, p. 27.

[44] An interpretation bolstered by Balkenhol's discourse around the "normalization" of public sculpture, in which he cites the work of Richard Serra as a case in point. See, "The Body is the Present", in *Witte de With, op. cit.*, p. 92.

back" not as a step backward, but as an avant-gardist action. This, apparently, is how Richard Armstrong's enthusiasm is to be taken: "One of the avant-garde's most important moves these past few years has been to recapture the portrait in art. Balkenhol is one of those who do it best. The portrait was a subject that had been taboo for a long time amongst advanced artists. Balkenhol's work is idealized — a portrait of anyone. A Mr. Average with a Mrs. Average at his side. He's standing up straight, his work is heroic[45]." In other words, the human figure's recovered "dignity" suited perfectly those who rejected abstraction and any form of expressionism — that of the generation of Lüpertz, Baselitz or Penck for example. The dominant theme then of Balkenhol's sculpture, in the artist's own words, is a double rejection of "the violence imposed by expressionism" and of the "rather dispassionate, rational, and very unsensual art of the seventies[46]." In saying this, the artist is fanning the flames of revenge, all the more strenuously as he is not entirely opposed to preceding generations. Lüpertz, most notably, has exploited the "already given" attitudes of classical statuary. "There is for instance the half-step of the Kouros," he explained in the mid-eighties. "The point is to figure out to what extent I'm

[45] Richard Armstrong, organizer of the exhibition *Carnegie International 1995*, interviewed by Yasuhide Fujio, *Atelier*, no.825, March 1996, p. 3. According to the interviewer, Balkenhol's work was pivotal to this exhibition where works from artists as different as Georg Baselitz, Franz West, Richard Armstrong or Cindy Sherman were shown.

[46] Stephan Balkenhol, Rochechouart 1994, p. 6; and comments taken from Benezra, "Stephan Balkenhol, The Figure as Witness", *Parkett*, n°. 36, pp. 37-40.

able to incorporate the new, the unusual, or even wounds[47]." If we compare Markus Lüpertz's *Shepherd* (1986) or, even more so, his *Ganymede* (two painted bronzes from 1985) to Balkenhol's *Man with Lamb* (painted wawa wood from 1996), we find the aggressiveness of the former is only rivaled by the serenity of the latter. It is less in the degrading usurpation of tradition that Balkenhol's specificity lies, than in the way he brings an old model up to date — right up to his using the hieratic smile of archaic Greek statuary. He thus treats tradition like he does his man/animal hybrids the seam remains invisible, and the reference to the past is completely assimilated into his characters' contemporaneousness. Lüpertz's disrespect, on the contrary, could be seen as stemming from the way he appropriates the past while allowing some of his loans to remain visible, creating some particularly conflicting combinations. On top of which, if Lüpertz sculpts like a painter (which is what he is after all), Balkenhol consciously sets himself apart from the rest of his generation by specifically defining himself as a sculptor, likening engravings to drawings in which color is subordinated: "I'm not a painter, and I don't really know much about color. [...] Obviously

[47] Markus Lüpertz, *in Raumbilder im Bronze: Per Kirkeby, Markus Lüpertz, A. R. Penck*, exhibition catalog, Kusthalle Bielfeld, 1986, p. 97, quoted by Kay Heymer, "Une sculpture de la ténacité et du refus", in *Skulptur, Baselitz, Immendorf, Kirkeby, Lüpertz, Penck*", Paris: Ed. de la différence, La Vue le Texte, I, 1989, p.82.

[48] "Woodwork is like drawing: it is predetermined by the format and dimensions of its support." Rochechouart 1994, p. 8; and on color, *Possible Worlds*, op. cit., p. 29. See also how Balkenhol distinguishes himself from Baselitz and Immendorf whose sculptures "cannot be understood without reference to their respective pictorial works", in his conversation with Philippe Vergne, *Parachute*, op. cit., p. 23.

color emphasizes sculptural qualities[48].” On this point, it is in going beyond what is specific to sculpture that Balkenhol gets back to the arguments of classical thought.

The use of color in sculpture as a means of adding a degree of realism has probably always been a preoccupation of artists. “Giacometti,” remembered Georges Boudaille upon the sculptor’s death, “had long spoken about his desire to do a sculpture in color. His dream was realism, total realism. [. .] He would move his face close to yours and whisper, ‘when I look at you like this, your face tapers and your body seems as thin as a twig.’ In the same way, he wanted to paint faces pink and hair brown. He went on about it incessantly. Anyhow, in Venice [in 1962] he couldn’t restrain himself any longer and before his retrospective was even completely set up, he started to paint his plaster casts. The effect was striking, troubling. But didn’t seem to trouble the jury which awarded him the grand prize for sculpture[49].” In so doing, the jury was probably only giving the sculptor’s gesture the place it was to keep within his work: that of an infatuation. In fact, the history of color in sculpture is a “vexed” one, to employ the term Clement Greenberg used with the intent to curtail its use. In the eighteenth century, Andreas Blühm points out, “Johan Joachim Winckelmann’s description of ancient statuary set the standards by which new and ancient sculpture was to be judged. The works Winckelmann had at his disposition were, in any case,

[49] Georges Boudaille, “L’interview impossible”, *Les lettres françaises*, n°. 1115, January 20 - 26, 1966, pp. 14-15.

either black [bronze] or white [marble], such that these norms themselves resulted from visual "restrictions" — even if rumors of antique polychromy were already beginning to spread [50]. Moreover, Winckelmann didn't view history with a neutral eye; he was looking for guidance in the present or, better still, the ratification of a (preconceived) ideal of beauty. One of his aesthetic principles was the clarity of the plastic form, which, of course, could be compromised by the use of color[51]." Beyond just establishing contemporary taste, the rejection of color was above all an attempt to define a timeless aesthetic norm, in opposition to a frivolous and ephemeral mask. To such an extent, as Michael Baxandall has shown in his study on wood sculpture in renaissance Germany, that "much of the bare wood sculpture one sees now is not monochrome sculpture... but polychrome sculpture which has lost its polychromy[52]." Rudolf Wittkower, retracing the history of the Horseman of Bamberg cathedral (1230/1240), suggests an eloquent example of how polychromy was suppressed. Indeed, with the exception of the crown, gilded right from the outset, the sculpture's bright colors had first been covered over, in the

[50] For more a more precise account of these "rumors", see the first chapter of John Gage's work, "The Classical Inheritance", *Colour and Culture, Practice and Meaning from Antiquity to Abstraction*, London: Thames and Hudson, 1993.

[51] Andreas Blühm, "In Living Color, A Short History of Color in Sculpture in the 19th Century", *The Color of Sculpture 1840/1910*, Amsterdam: Van Gogh Museum, July 26 - November 17, 1996, p. 12. The author refers to J. J. Winckelmann, *Geschichte der Kunst des Altertums* (1763 - 1768), Vienna: Ludwig Goldscheider, 1934, p. 61.

[52] Michael Baxandall, *The Limewood Sculptors of Renaissance Germany*, New Haven and London: Yale University Press, 1980, p. 48.

seventeenth century, with a whitewash; then, at the beginning of the nineteenth century, a corrosive restoring agent lifted both this discreet veil and the original colors with it, laying the stone bare[53]. More recently, Clement Greenberg, who in 1940 penned a "newer" Laocoon, could not feign ignorance of the polychrome sculpture tradition. Questioned late in his life on hybrid works of painting and sculpture, his reasoning appeared to rely on the old strategy of banishing polychromy by admitting its use. "These hybrids in my experience have rarely achieved success. [...] [Anne Truitt] painted her boxes; when the color worked it was good, when the color didn't work it wasn't good. [...] You know, the Greeks painted their sculptures. In the Acropolis museum, the *korai*, the female figures, show enough traces of paint because they had been buried when the Persians invaded Greece, and they were not dug up again because they were thought too old-fashioned. So they were preserved with the color. And the color works, they're better with the color than without. But most Greek sculpture that has come down to us is just bronze or stone. You can't generalize here. Everything is specific[54]." In short, polychromy is definitely marginal, and one should steer clear of its influence. In fact, right from Greek statuary onwards, polychromy could apparently only be justified, for Greenberg and for his predecessors, within a monochrome system to which it was subordinated. Thus the

53 Rudolf Wittkower, *Sculpture: Processes and Principles*, London: 1977.

54 Clement Greenberg, "A Public Debate with Clement Greenberg" (University of Ottawa, March 30, 1987), in Thierry de Duve, *Clement Greenberg Between the Lines,* Paris: Dis Voir, 1996, p.145.

violent denial of the use of color in antiquity was followed, in the nineteenth century, by taking into account contradictory elements. The strategy was founded on the strength of an observation: "Most often, the hair and beards of the figures, as well as the reins of the horses were painted red or red-brown, while the face (with the exception of the eyes and eyebrows), arms, legs, and animals' bodies remained uncolored, allowing the marble to work to full effect[55]." It is clearly within the confines of this narrow, tightly monitored space that color operates in Balkenhol's work — in his human figures at any rate. The color is not expressive and accentuates the distinctness of the material without pushing the kinship of its natural color to that of skin to the point of mistaking the wood for what it was supposed to be representing. In this framework, texture can even function as a rampart against illusion. Yet Balkenhol admits that just a couple of slips can lead to the wood's "disappearance"[56]. Seen in this way, with the help of distance, the whole is apt — whatever the sculptor may say to the contrary — to deceive the viewers senses, pulling him into its play of illusion. An illusion against which Balkenhol protests too energetically to have brought it about himself naively.

It could be said that the work attracts the public, even giving viewers the pleasure of immediate recognition, without deluding them. But the sculptor is uncomfortable even with this kind of

55 Wolfgang Drost, "Color, Sculpture, Mimesis, A Nineteenth Century Debate", *The Colour of Sculpture 1840 - 1910*, op. cit., p.62.
56 Stephan Balkenhol, *Possible Works*, op. cit., p. 29.

seduction: “I’m not ssufficiently up front with myself concerning seduction. It’s a fact that the visual or the aesthetic sometimes has a power we can’t control. In a certain sense, it is a moral duty to use it to good ends, but I don’t want to be a moralist[57]!” Balkenhol is thus suspicious of both seduction and of any moralism proscribing too much seduction; in other words, of a tendency to distinguish moral pleasure (the only real end of art) from superficial physical pleasure. Seduction, of course, functions through color, whose presence may overwhelm the senses. Greenberg, arguing against such excess, wrote that “had they been monochrome, [Truitt’s] ‘objects would have qualified as first examples of orthodox Minimal Art. And with the help of monochrome the artist would have been able to dissemble her feminine sensibility… as so many masculine Minimalists have *their* rather feminine sensibilities.” By the same token, David Smith also met with reproach for his dubious penchant for sensuality. “Polished or painted surfaces might in particular instances, if not in others, attract the eye too much, and the attracted eye lingers, while the unattracted eye hastens toward the essential. […] For all that, the question of color in the Smith’s art (as in all recent sculpture along the same lines) remains a vexed one[58].” The problem for all intents and purposes is the same whether it is abstraction or figuration which is at issue —

[57] Stephan Balkenhol, Rochechouart 1994, p. 14.
[58] Clement Greenberg, “Changer: Anne Truitt”, *The Collected Essays and Criticism*, vol. 4, John O’Brian (ed.), Chicago: University of Chicago Press, 1993, p.290; and on David Smith, “David Smith’s New Sculpture”, *ibid.*, p.191-192.

it essentially depends on the will to recognize, and obey, the limits set on this kind of aesthetic. Balkenhol has himself tested out the perverse effects of a seduction which makes the specific limits he has set on his realism give way. "I try," says Balkenhol in this respect, "not to delude the viewer, but sometimes I notice that people are so used to lies that they automatically feel taken in[59]." Neal Benezra recalls the violent reactions brought about by the exhibition of one of Balkenhol's works, *Man on a Buoy* (painted oak and metal, 250 x 50 x 40 cm) on the Thames in February 1992. An article, under the ambiguous title, "Why can't you dummies just let me alone?", by *Evening Standard* reporter Robin Stringer gave the following account of events: "A sculptured figure moored in the Thames off the National Theatre, part of a contemporary art show on the South Bank, has proved a little too lifelike for some caring Londoners. Not only have they contacted security officers at the theatre and called police, but several have attempted to go to his rescue. One even leapt into the river reportedly shouting 'Don't jump' and had to be rescued himself by the River Police, while the wooden statue looked on unmoved. [...] At the suggestion of the River Police, the Port of London authority has now moved it from its original mooring, a buoy on which the figure looked particularly precarious, and put it on a much larger and safer-looking pontoon which rides higher in the water[60]."

[59] Stephan Balkenhol, Rochechouart 1994, p. 14.

[60] Quoted by Neal Benezra, Washington 1995, p. 23; the *Evening Standard* article, from February 28, 1992, is reproduced as fig. 1.

In this particular case, the public was up against a work whose realism, no longer keeping the sensations it engendered at a distance, went beyond its own limits. Through the use of a distancing effect, canceling out the effects of the wood's texture and the presence of a plinth, the realism of Balkenhol's art trapped the viewers. It literally confused sculpture with its spectator by giving life to what was supposed to be, at most, only a vehicle of an illusion aware of its own limits. In this sense, the *Evening Standard* reporter's choice of the word "Dummy" was particularly astute, bringing out in the article's title all its various levels of meaning: from puppet to double agent to idiot. The latter, evidently, applied to the poor fool who nearly drowned. On a second level, the title's exclamation comes straight from the mouth of the sculpture itself (notwithstanding that a dummy is mute) and is insultingly directed at potential rescuers. For there is no doubt that the confused situation in which everything was out of place was indeed tantamount to an insult that could only be rectified by the forces of law and order: by putting the various "dummies" back to the place where they belonged, and turning the plinth into a pontoon.

This anecdote, though not unique in Balkenhol's work[61], may seem trivial and inappropriate in an analysis of his work. It is, after all, not generally recommended to take these sorts of marginal phenomena seriously — for the simple reason that they are borderline. And yet it is apparently in these problematic margins

[61] See Neal Benezra, Washington 1995, p. 32.

of representation that the contradictions of Balkenhol's art are located. The artist claims to want "everything at once", but then right away feels the need to moderate such excess: "sensuality; expression, but not too much; liveliness, but no superficial garrulousness; momentaneousness, but no anecdotes; wit, but no corny jokes; self-irony, but no cynicism[62]." In this way, Balkenhol finds himself trapped in the jaws of a tradition demanding that the artist control his means of expression, that he set out his intentions clearly, and that he be able to resolve every contradiction. Which is why his remarks may at times give the impression of a somewhat forced justification. Clearly, Balkenhol's theoretical discourse doesn't so much deal explicitly with his work, as it shifts according to the contradictions engendered by his sculptures. Thus, referring to the incident of the figure on the Thames, and discussing this borderline case where figurative representation crosses over into simulacrum, Balkenhol instinctively — but somewhat strangely — fell back upon Giacometti's conception of "realism"; that is of a representation which seeks out resemblance under the skin of appearances[63]. Yet his sculpting in mass blocks clearly bears little relation to the organic process of modeling clay or plaster, fleshing out — but scarcely at all — fragile figures, like Giacometti. One encounters a similar incongruity when emphasizing the "generic" character of Balkenhol's figures: the artist promptly brings up the conflicting fact of the living models used for some of his female

[62] Stephan Balkenhol, "Notes by Stephan Balkenhol, 1992", *About Men and Sculpture*, op. cit., p. 16.
[63] In conversation with the author, June 15, 1997.

figures. In pointing out that he is just as apt to start right in on the wood mass as to draw some guidelines on one side of the block, to select a wood for its qualities or allow himself to be guided by his materials, Balkenhol obviously tries to avoid getting trapped in any system whatsoever. When he mentions Giacometti, it brings to mind a more sensitive remark made by Jean Genet in the sculptor's studio. "Their beauty — Giacometti's sculptures seem to be held in this incessant, uninterrupted back and forth movement between the most extreme distance and the closest familiarity: this oscillation is never ending and it is in this way that they can be said to be in movement[64]."

Looking at Balkenhol's renewal of "the tradition of public sculpture", Neal Benezra has affirmed that "not since Claes Oldenburg has a sculptor so successfully employed deadpan humor to draw people to art[65]." However, if one opposes only an ironic consciousness of tradition to a critique of his conservatism, it is possible to appreciate the positive values of his "insult" which, in some ways, does "bring people to art" — even if it means their drowning. Balkenhol, however, isn't looking to insult anyone, but rather to integrate public resistance like a more or less determinant parameter in the language used by a given art. "This language," he says, "has to be a medium for understanding, but of course every artist has to decide on his own grammar. So it is always new and you

[64] Jean Genet, *L'Atelier d'Alberto Giacometti*, Marc Barbezat - L'arbalète, 1958 -1963, n.p.
[65] See Neal Benezra, Washington 1995, p. 23.

always have to refer to conventions, otherwise there is no understanding possible. But of course, you have to question these conventions[66]." In this language game, Balkenhol takes conventions for what they are: words whose meaning always ends up slipping. It seems that Balkenhol stands on the same tenuous ground as his figures, oscillating between consensual understanding, leading to a form of stasis or muteness, and an insulting incomprehension — provoking a sometimes violent reaction. Balkenhol's sculpture is perhaps based upon this tension, and upon leading us to reflect on "man and mankind, thinking, history and philosophy and (...) what mimesis should be[67]." This tension is perhaps tenable only if the artist himself becomes a dummy, this time in the sense of a "person secretly acting for another while apparently representing his or her interests": the double agent of tradition and subversion.

[66] Stephan Balkenhol, "The Body is the Present", *Witte de With, The Lectures*, op. cit., p. 92.
[67] Ibid., p. 96.

## *The Living Sound of Wood: Stephan Balkenhol's Neo-expressionless Sculpture*

*For me the noise of Time is not sad: I love bells, clocks, watches — and I recall that at first photographic implements were related to techniques of cabinetmaking and the machinery of precision: cameras, in short, were clocks for seeing, and perhaps in me someone very old still hears in the photographic mechanism the living sound of the wood.*

Roland Barthes, *Camera Lucida: Reflections on Photography*, 1980.[1]

### *Shortcuts*

A woman driving on the highway through a forest passes a pair of giants. Statues of Paul Bunyan, the legendary lumberjack, and his blue ox, Babe, are common roadside attractions in North America. And even though they are big banalities, the woman later confesses that she could not resist turning around for a good look as she sped by and they disappeared into the distance. What she especially remembers are Paul's pants: ridiculously large on his

[1]Roland Barthes, *Camera Lucida: Reflections on Photography*, New York: Hill & Wang, 1980, p. 15.

trunk-like legs. She says that more than anything, this is what reminded her of the work of Stephan Balkenhol. For it too incites a reactionary double-take, and produces a similar, disconcerting feeling of fondness for figurative sculpture, so seemingly *retardataire*, conceptually and materially, in this post-modern period. (Another artist friend, less kindly disposed, hedged his admiration for the work with a dark premonition of the critical death of Balkenhol, consequent to the work being overtaken by the artist's increasing technical facility, combined with a certain sweetness of vision and, most damning, its popularity — an audience's affection for all those carved men, women, animals — especially the penguins.)

There is nothing dark or dangerous or, to use that most authoritative password of contemporary art, "difficult" about Stephan Balkenhol's work and, for some reason, this makes us nervous. For my own part, I would add a writer's self-consciousness at over-determining a body of work that seems remarkably void of ambiguity or complexity. On the other hand, it seems it is precisely because of its straightforward appeal for permission to do so that Balkenhol's art situates itself so nicely and with such conviction in relation to historical and contemporary art. What reveals itself as surprising, given the instant familiarity of the work, its imagery and themes, is the breadth of issues upon which it touches, gently but firmly. This essay allows Stephan Balkenhol's almost alarmingly tidy art to become a bit unravelled.

*Permissions*

In interviews, Balkenhol is direct and completely at ease with his practice, not in the least bit embattled by his position. A student of Ulrich Rückreim, whose hewn stone sculptures carry all the weight of minimalist abstraction, Balkenhol says he studied hard to "arrive at a kind of work that allows the figurative image to appear once again."[2] Erasing any touches of rebellion, he adds, "but I don't know if I would have reached this point without Rückreim," crediting his teacher with having grounded his art firmly in the fundamental issues of the day. Documented in a pair of photographs taken out side, *Eisskulptur* (with M. Bourgeois, 1980) is a competent exercise in conceptualism. In the first photo, a folding chair made of clear plastic is standing out-of-doors, next to a throne-like seat made of ice, which is covered in a canvas drop-cloth. Time passes, the temperature changes, and in the second photograph, the ice throne vanishes. Having melted away, leaving its wrap in a puddle, like a model's discarded drapery, its remains lying next to the plastic chairs, which is, of course still standing. Another early work is almost pure minimalism: a granite trough with a hose at one end fills with water. Reaching a certain level, the water empties in a spigot-like stream through a hole drilled out of the opposite end. This fountain also happens to be a monument to rural technology, as this is the way farmers keep the fresh water

[2] All Stephan Balkenhol quotes are cited from the interview (June 1994) with Alexandra Midal in the exhibition catalogue of the Musée Départmental de Rochechouart, 1994.

flowing for their animals in the fields, who gather to drink at the trough. It is interesting to note the presence of water in the ice sculpture and the stone block, melting and flowing through these two important lessons in seventies sculpture.

Balkenhol's first figures appeared in 1983 in the form of single men and women, attached to their pedestals, and posed in the nude. Like Adam and Eve expelled from Eden, the figures soon adopted the habit of dress. For the most part, Balkenhol now carves them clothed in pants, shirts, dresses, shoes — ordinary attire that casts his people out of the past's timeless world of myths and allegories, out of academic sculptor's ateliers, and situates them in the present, where, as the sculptor points out, we don't typically encounter one another naked. It's no less of a paradise: animals, for example, are plentiful. Birds, beasts, reptiles, fish, all have a place on a plinth in Balkenhol's art. Another classical touch is the use of polychrome. Hair, nipples, eyes, outfits, stand out, stained in colors, against the naked, clear flesh, which tends to remain uncolored, except in those very rare instances when non-whites are involved.

The sculptures' skins (furs, feathers, scales, flesh) are not cold and smooth — marmoreal as classical sculpture — not ice, not stone, but wood, and roughly hewn wood at that. Crudely chipped out of blocks of wood, Balkenhol's sculptures reveal all of their imperfections, such as cracks and knots, particularly at their bases, which tend to be relatively unsculpted, left like stumps and trunks, boards or posts. These sculptures' surfaces and volumes throw obvious connective lines back to Rückreim, which Balkenhol picks up. As open signs of process and unapologetic truths as to the nature of his materials, these attributes belong to the contemporary tradition with which he allies himself. As personal references he points to Rodin, Picasso and Giacometti, sculptors whose work epitomizes classic modernism, and to their historic sources in Egyptian, Roman and Greek art. He seems less comfortable with, in fact adamantly opposed to, evocations of an explicitly national tradition, namely German Expressionism, that inevitably come up in discussions of his art. He says with evident distaste, "A crying or laughing person is petrified in that expression. I prefer to leave an open space for the imaginary; that gives force to the sculpture. I don't much care for the violence imposed by expressionism." The faces of his people are set in relaxed neutrality, as pleasantly unperturbed as animals at rest. This makes for a curious exchange: instead of anthropomorphizing his animals, attributing them with human intelligence, emotion, or expression, Balkenhol is inclined to bring out the placid beast-like qualities of his human subjects.

Rejecting the "violence of expressionism," Balkenhol renders his figures emotional blanks, in order that they function as passive receptacles for whatever responses individual viewers will impose upon them. He describes the perfect encounter between viewer and sculpture as being comparable to a brush with a stranger, uncompromisingly anonymous and, at the same time, intensely vivid.

"It's a little as though you found a private photo in the street: you don't know the person or persons in the picture and yet at the same time, it's something very personal. My sculptures can represent a definite person or whoever, a 'Mr. Everyman.'" There is one recurrent figure in Balkenhol's cast of characters, who comes across as being just that person: a pleasant-looking man with a white shirt, black pants and brown hair, an idealized self-portrait of the sculptor perhaps. He seems to have been there from the beginning of Balkenhol's figurative art and turns up everywhere (like the Maidenform Woman), singularly (he appeared implacably bobbing up and down in the middle of the Thames as the *Man on a Buoy* in a public installation of 1992) and in multiples (he was only recently triplicated for one huge work that had each man's arms making a slightly different gesture that radically changed his entire demeanor.) We've seen him depicted in arrested states of development, as a young man, a younger man, an adolescent, a boy, all standing round each other, back-to-back, with pedestals joined into one big stage. (Balkenhol has, as yet, never sculpted an old person or an infant.) We've seen him with his shirt off. And now he has just shown up in miniature, in another group of three like men in white shirts, aping the mime "See No, Hear No, Speak No Evil": the quintessential state of denial embodied by the Everyman, who absorbs everyone's impressions without ever actually expressing himself.

Another German artist who has used expressionless-ness to great effect is August Sander, the photographer whose life-long project entailed a collection of Weimar-period physiognomies, organized by profession, and documented through portraiture. Butchers, bakers, philosophers, farmers, lawyers, doctors, musicians, politicians, tailors, painters, sculptors, and, in a non-working class of their own, idiots, are some of those who posed for Sander's camera, faces forward with features voided of expression[3]. Sitters were instructed to look at the camera without smiling, wincing or frowning, relinquishing any individual expectations for the session, in order to submit to and receive signification through the photographer's larger project. As with Balkenhol's figures, the people in Sander's pictures become receptacles (or what Katharina Fritsch calls "vases") for, first the artist, then the viewer's projections[4]. The results then are not intended to show individuals, but types.

[3] Begun in 1910 and containing approximately 540 images, *Citizens of the Twentieth Century* was Sander's attempt to present what he called the "existing social order" of contemporary Germany, which he saw as being cyclical, starting with "earthbound men," rising up to "representatives of the highest civilization", and dipping "back again to the idiot." Sander's was not an unusual project for its day, as Ulrich Keller points out. After Germany lost the First World War there was a sudden glut of caricatures and photographs of German people and places appearing in print in magazines, books, newspapers, and pamphlet forms as if in answer to an unspoken demand for imagery upon which to reconstruct a new national identity. Patriotic primers such as *Germany 1914-1924: A Book of Greatness and Hope* and photo-albums of famous *People of the Time: One Hundred and One Photos from Present-Day Germany* were "intended to give the public the comforting impression that the German spirit had survived the war uninjured and that, at least in the cultural sector, the 'land of poets and thinkers' still played a leading role in the world." See Ulrich Keller, *August Sander: Citizens of the Twentieth Century*, Cambridge: MIT Press, 1980 (1986 edition), p. 9.

[4] Of course, an important difference between Balkenhol's and Sander's representations rests with the subject. Unlike the photographer, the sculptor works without an actual model before him; he draws his figures as if out of thin air.

In 1929, a selection of sixty of Sander's portraits was published as *Antlitz der Zeit (Face of the Time)*. The book failed to sell as well as anticipated, perhaps because the faces were so blank in a market driven by the need for subjective expressions of Germany's greatness. Compared to Sander's book of almost passport-style subjects, publications such as Helmar Lerski's *Everyday Heads* (1931) and Erna Lendvai-Dircksen's *German Folk Faces* (1930) showed ordinary citizens posed for maximum heroic effect, exhibiting arresting profiles, handsome three-quarter turns, with determined, pious, stoical and noble expressions capable of demonstrating that no matter how rustic, backwards or down-trodden, Germany was headed for a strong future[5].

Sander's work was deemed by one conservative critic to be "not a document of uplift, [or] enthusiasm", and was confiscated by the Nazis.[6] The rise of the Third Reich ended the greatest collecting phase of the *Citizens* project, and though Sander continued to refine it throughout the rest of his life, he focussed his later efforts on organizing the existing archive into albums, only occasionally adding new portraits. In the meantime, the face of the times had changed so dramatically that it was difficult in any case for Sander to continue with his original human panorama. During the war he

[5] Pictures by Sander's colleagues, such as Lendvai-Dircksen were now turning up in the Stoedtner Picture Agency's archive of "Heads of the German Racial and National Community" being compiled for newspapers, publishers, schools, and Nazi training courses. Ulrich Keller, *op. cit.*, p. 19

[6] *Ibid*, p. 19

pointed his camera at landscapes instead, first at historic Cologne and then at the Rheinlands[7].

Even more neutral than his physiognomic documents, the landscape would seem to have been politically beyond reproach. (Nevertheless he was forced to abandon the Cologne project when the Nazis confiscated the pictures of what they perceived to be strategic military sites.) For contemporary artists coming out post-war Germany and entering the scene in the 1960s, the landscape as subject seems to have had a similar value, this time for both a national and an international audience, in conflict about German identity since the holocaust. Bernd and Hilla Becher's documentary series of industrial and architectural landscapes might be seen as picking up where Sander's wartime production left off, producing photographs that are conspicuously neutral in both style and subject matter. (Since Re-unification, the question of German identity appears even more accentuated as East Germany's history must now be incorporated.) And when Becher's students, such as Andreas Gursky, Thomas Ruff and Thomas Struth, many of whom also started out by taking pictures of architecture, earned from their teacher's legacy, (as Balkenhol earned from Rückreim) permission to depict the figure, their subjects appear as passive types, faces wiped clean of expression, as facades. As different as Ruff's photograph of a young man (brown

[7] A book was published based on the latter, but Sander never realized his ultimate project of constructing a portrait of the cultured landscape, uniquely shaped by particular people in a specific time and space.

hair, traces of a beard, pronounced forehead and Adam's apple) is from Balkenhol's carved sculpture of a slightly older, but still youthful Everyman, both artists have actively represented looks of abstraction on their subjects' faces. There is no violence of expression, laughing or crying, leaving the viewer free to project, or not, upon these impartial faces. Thus in distancing himself from Expressionism, Balkenhol's sculpture unexpectedly participates in Germany's postwar photographic legacy. Even his highly developed sense of craftsmanship finds precedence there.

Whenever he discussed his work, August Sander emphasized "three basic concepts: See, observe and think correctly!" He was not impressed by the rakish angling and cropping that took place in, say Läszlö Moholy-Nagy's avant-garde compositions. And despite having been one of its early adherents, Sander sounded especially intolerant of what he saw as the obfusticating trickery of such techniques as soft-focus and double exposure that took place in the name of "art photography". In his mature work, Sander aimed at documentation, which he equated with a kind of craftsman-like honesty. He held the camera at waist height, pointed it at his subject, and took the picture. In a series of radio lectures given in 1931, Sander demonstrated himself to be a keen observer of photography's history. Like Old Kingdom Egyptian art, photography's first historic period was also its golden age. According to Keller, Sander lauded the daguerreotype as "the peak of craftsmanship in the evolution of the medium."[8] Thinking back on photography's past also led Roland

[8] Ibid, p. 18

Barthes to reflect on its early craftsmanship, the "techniques of cabinet making" that went into making a camera. These early days also essentially coincide with one of photography's most self-reflexive moments as its various authors struggled to reconcile whether the new medium was a product of nature or of culture. Was it a scientific form of documentation, or an artistically driven medium? In one famous tract, Henry Fox Talbot, who photographed both botanical studies and hand-writing, dubbed it "The Pencil of Nature," leaving the options open as to which discipline — science or art — would own the new medium.[9]

Together these metaphors establish a site, invitingly littered with wood chips and shavings, tools and pencils (there's the smell of resin, of wood stains and dry paper in the air) for further consideration of Balkenhol's work in terms of photography. His sculpture begins with the pencil, drawing directly on wood the image that he will carve into shape. The finished works can even be compared to pencils, when they've been hand-sharpened, leaving a precious point atop a whittled shaft. A photograph of a work in progress in the studio shows this process underway. A massive post stands partially hacked away by a chainsaw, leaving a blocky silhouette. Upon it is sketched a man with his head turned slightly to the left and his hands thrust into his pants' pockets. His is an alert presence, that of a thinking man, a cultured man, in sharp

[9] cf. Geoffrey Batchen, *Burning with Desire: The Conception of Photography*, Cambridge: MIT Press, 1997.

contrast to the crude volume. (In the end, when the man is carved and painted, the unelaborated shape of the pedestal will serve as a reminder of the sculpture's first form by keeping the foot of the sculpture permanently planted in the studio.) To see the work in this state is to see that adage of traditional sculptors, from scrimshaw artists to Phidias to Constantin Brancusi, who talk about releasing the image that already exists inside the lump of raw material. One might also, alternatively, or by extension, see a picture developing, particularly against this backdrop. In Balkenhol's studio, hanging behind the unfinished standing man is one of his *Kopfrelief*, a portrait head on big square board, composed like a giant photograph, snapped in wood. *(Fifty-seven Penguins* (1991) comprises fifty-seven snap-shots, each bird observed in wood, caught in a different pose.)

"Wood is my material of predilection", Balkenhol says, because it requires a rhythm of work that I find agreeable." As evinced from the surfaces of his sculptures, uniformly hacked away over time in quick even strokes, the rhythm appears to be that of a clock, such as Roland Barthes noticed when he considered old cameras, imagined "the machinery of precision" and heard "the living sound of wood." Balkenhol's process is also subtractive, like lapsed minutes, taking away the increments, then leaving an image that must be experienced as an object in real time and space. Here the photograph goes its own way, on a separate course from Balkenhol's sculpture. The photographic image is wedged into a moment in the past, constantly pulling the viewer backwards to that time, never fully coming to rest in the present. This is an important distinction, since it is sculpture's concrete and temporal reality that attracts Balkenhol. By way of this distinction, he claims to be less interested in painting for "always [being] more conceptual, it creates an imaginary reality in the image being represented." Aside from the time element, however, photography is again called into consideration when the sculptor claims for his art the aim of objectivity. (Objectivity may be one of photography's most debased claims; nonetheless it remains photography's special precinct in the realm of representation.) "In my work as a sculptor, I try to use this physical presence to evoke a reality in the viewer's imagination. In this way the reality is embodied." He clarifies his representations by claiming, "I believe that my sculptures are objective."

One of the strongest afterimages produced by Balkenhol's sculptures is of an object that is part tree, part creature. It is as if the pedestals sprouted the figures that rise from them, like fresh shoots from old or dead wood. By leaving the bases relatively unsculpted, Balkenhol keeps one foot in the studio, the other in the forest. The Blackforest, the ur-woods of German culture is teeming with speculators: story-tellers, philosophers, musicians, novelists and artists, who all have a foot in the imaginative power of the forest. In a manner of seeing, Martin Heideigger forged this connection into an image of an essential link between peasant culture and the earth, which he found and celebrated in a work by Vincent van Gogh, a painting of two empty shoes. Meyer Schapiro, in turn, responded by arguing that they were, in fact, in terms of Heideigger's appreciation, emblematic of all the shoes that had been emptied by the Nazis in their infamous attachment to the Fatherland, the Earth. Stepping outside this debate, and returning to *Citizens of the Twentieth Century*, August Sander, one recalls, began his picture cycle with farmers and peasants, with "earth-bound men".[10]

### *Trespasses*

Another sound is echoed in the "living sound of wood" and that is the (ch-chunk, ch-chunk, ch-chunk) rhythm of the printing press, of mechanical reproduction. In his discussion of historic precedents for Sander's portrait atlas, Ulrich Keller observes that awkward moment in publishing history when the cost of reproducing photographic images was prohibitive enough to require that photos be translated into woodcuts, or other forms of engraving for printing purposes.[11] (Looking even further backwards, long before photography, he cites Jost Ammann's *Kunstbüchlein*, a Renaissance book of portrait engravings of public figures, as one of the earliest examples of Sander's project.) Cursively carved, shaggy with burrs of curling wood and soaked with pigment, Balkenhol's sculptures

[10] For himself, Balkenhol insists that his choice of wood has nothing to do with romanticism of the forest, pointing out that he obtains his materials in an industrial context, from lumber yards where wood is stocked as raw material.
[11] Ulrich Keller, *op. cit.*, p. 25.

are, in a manner of seeing, three dimensional printer's blocks for woodcut engravings. And though they are not used to make impressions, they relate directly to works on paper. Drawing plays an important role in Balkenhol's art. Not only does he sketch directly on wood to determine where he will cut and what he will carve out of it, but he also uses drawing as an autonomous medium. The line is quick, abrupt, making his drawings more into sketches or cartoons than finished renderings. As is clear in the subject matter, Balkenhol clearly enjoys the way drawing on paper "allows you to treat subjects that would be impossible to handle otherwise." He has made drawings in which a globe with female features purses her lips; or, a hybrid is born: part man, part washing machine; even that monument of classicism, the Laocoon suddenly becomes a do-able appropriation, when it's been reduced to the scraggly subject of a quick sketch. And even when he's wielding a chain saw, Balkenhol's sculpture appears as a form of sketching. Perhaps this approach is another form of permission, by which the artist grants himself the right to represent the figure; the artist is not necessarily sculpting, but *drawing* in wood. Wood imparts a sense of familiarity that makes it practically ordinary. As Balkenhol points out, "its connotations are not so strong as those of stone or bronze. It's more neutral, somewhat related to paper."

Surveying Balkenhol's sculpture of the past decade, one can almost measure his skills improving, from the first relatively crude nudes to the current figures who appear to pose according to the sculptors bidding. Wood offers less and less resistance to whatever plans his pencil sketches. With limber grace, a figure bends over at the waist and stares at the viewer from between his legs. Balkenhol is now literally drawing in wood. He has perfected his craft, a craft which speaks of hours spent handling tools and materials, honing skills not generally associated with contemporary life. Figurative wood carving belongs to Renaissance and Medieval art, when artists were, for the most part, anonymous artisans who decorated utilitarian objects and architecture. Balkenhol says he encountered his earliest influences as a child in a catholic family visiting churches and cathedrals, where carved sculpture is typically an integral part of the overall symbolic structure. To encounter as one does in Balkenhol's art a similar form of craft, functioning automously (without walls or handles) is to experience the pleasant surprise of seeing an obsolete technology not only work, but work well with renewed possibilities.

Another pleasure of Balkenhol's art comes in its imagery, which is also a product of its rusticity, making it look like toys. German craftsmen are highly regarded for their figurative wood carving. In the story of the Nutcracker, what is the treasured gift which Herr Drosselmeyer presents to Clara, battled over by all the children, but a carved wooden Nutcracker in the shape of a little man? Balkenhol freely acknowledges associations with toy-making in his work when he bottoms off his sculpture of a man's head and trunk with a rounded ball (instead of legs), and attaches him to a pedestal, out of reach of children. Toy figures can be seen as dolls, but also as puppets, which seems the stronger association for

Balkenhol's men and women, even though there are no strings attached. In writing *On the Marionette Theater* in 1810, Heinrich von Kleist observed a peculiar exchange between animals and humans from which he extrapolates to describe the powerful hold that puppets have on people: "We see that in the organic world, to the extent that reflection grows dimmer and weaker, the grace therein becomes more brilliant and powerful."[12] Rigid, still and plain, bearing only the dimmest relation to real flesh and blood, Balkenhol's sculpture seems to have a share of this power to abstract vital identification from the viewer. Made of wood, they have enormous grace as human presences, which, perversely, gives way to what might be the only tinge of darkness in his art. For grace is an attribute of physical agility and poise, and also of a moral state of innocence. In Balkenhol's sculpture strong associations with childhood (animals, puppets, toys) are not altogether appropriate for figures of a certain age. In the grips of this uneasy fit, an adult's expressionless face can read as a sign of absence of experience, or an unconscionable spirit. "Of course", says one of von Kleist's characters ruminating on the untarnished brilliance of a marionette performance, "the spirit cannot err when there is none." Especially when they are clustered into groups, Balkenhol's figures can generate for one split second a terrible sense of soullessness.

[12] Quoted in: *Fragments for a History of the Human Body, Part One*, Michel Feher, ed., New York: Zone, 1989, p. 420.

*Expressionist/Expressionless*

Balkenhol may eschew German Expressionism as a source for his art, and yet connections remain to be discussed. They begin on a graphic level. I open a book of German art at random and come to a 1924 sketch The lines in Expressionist drawing, hacked out in slashing rhythms harken back with Balkenhol to similar historic points, in late medieval and renaissance German art, when the printing press was first starting to mechanically churn out images. (One might even see the roughly carved and stained surfaces of Balkenhol's sculpture as wood-printing blocks in the round.) Expressionism is thought of mostly in terms of print-making and painting, but there is a small and significant body of sculpture — figurative imagery carved in wood and painted in opaque colors — which goes a long way towards bridging the gap left by the "violence of expression," which Balkenhol patently rejects. Treated as an experimental medium, like drawing, its lineage and function were distinguished from painting. As E.L. Kirchner enthused in a letter to a collector, "It is so good for painting and drawing, this making of figures, it lends wholeness to drawing and is such a sensual pleasure when blow by blow the figure grows more and more from the trunk. There is a figure in every trunk, one must only peel it out."[13]

Most of the Expressionist membership toyed in wood at some point in their careers. However Kirchner's involvement was the

[13] Kirchner to Gustav Schiefler, 1911, quoted in Stephanie Barron, *German Expressionist Sculpture*, exhib. cat., Los Angeles County Museum of Art, p. 23.

most extensive and telling. After Die Brücke formally dissolved, Kirchner retreated to Frauenkirch in 1918, near Davos, Switzerland. He set up household in his *Haus in den LÑrchen*, which he completely furnished with carved Swiss pine furniture and decorative objects. He carved the doors, a tray, a bed, a mirror frame, a chest, the chairs. In celebration of his new surroundings, he carved figures based on agrarian life, a horse, a farmer, a cow. *Kuh* (1920-23), an unlikely expressionistic subject, is docile and doe-eyed, painted, like most Expressionist sculpture, with details and markings. Made primarily for private enjoyment in a domestic context, Kirchner's wooden sculptures are decorative in feeling, more contained in their expression than his paintings. They contribute as props to a utopian dream of artists living in self-imposed exile, after the Polynesian odysseys of Gauguin (whose carved sculpture and ceramics were as admired by the Expressionists as his travels). Emil Nolde's forays into sculpture occurred on board ship in 1913-14, en route to his South Sea adventures. In all craftsman-like honesty, he says of the hand-sized figures that he carved, "I just tried to get a little beauty out of the firewood."[14] He linked their production to the sense of time he experienced on the ocean voyage in a "vegetative calm," the slow rhythm of which he found registered best in wood. Not all the Expressionists downplayed their sculpture to this extent. Heckel threw himself bodily into overcoming the resistance of wood, producing an important

[14] Ibid., Nolde quoted p. 163.

group of works. By-and-large, however, it was a secondary realm of production compared to the movement's primary modes of expression, which remained painting and printmaking. As such, it afforded an opportunity to openly explore the guises that most compelled them: the primitive, the craftsman, the anonymous maker of things. Much Expressionist sculpture is made to be subordinated by architecture or some other larger scheme or design, with the makers adopting the humble pose of unknown guild-members decorating the cathedral, the niche, the newel post. Painting on canvas, modernism's quintessential art form, and made for showing almost competitively in galleries and salons, could never grant such permission.

What might have, for the Expressionists, been only a slight distinction between sculpture and painting creates a broad margin today. It admits Balkenhol, who has invested in some of Expressionism's most traditional aspects and quirks, without relegating him as a contemporary artist to the Neo-expressionist movement. Comparatively speaking, the Neo-expressionist sculpture of Georg Baselitz reads more like a wooden version of Expressionist painting, with a kind of commanding authority and personal bravado that makes it relatively unlike historic Expressionist sculpture. Neo-expressionism is the connection that doesn't jibe with Balkenhol's work, and one hears his attempts to distance himself from the modern movement more convincingly as an expression of his determination not be associated with its Post-modern rendition.

And yet, in giving these peers wide berth, Balkenhol enters into what is potentially a more loaded realm of latent national identity. When Baselitz, Kiefer, and their colleagues returned to the Expressionist tradition in the 1980s, there was the thrill of a taboo being broken in returning to a figurative imagery haunted by a shameful and troublesome national identity, which is collectively the subject of their art. During the second World War, however, Expressionism, which had already been supplanted by Neue Sachlichkeit as an avant-garde movement, was banned by The Third Reich as "Degenerate." (The Fascists favored a form of classicism based on the figure that was sapped of any sign of individual expression, and, with it, any traces of humanity as well.) Outside the Reich, Expressionism was upheld internationally by exiled dealers and curators as an established tradition of *good* German culture, of anti-Nazi art. So that in a strange but historic sense, it's the expressionless figure that today conveys the more disturbing image. Not for of any proposed semblance to Nazi kitsch, or even because of the war specifically, but because the deadpan figure is a complicated, disconcerting image of ambivalence, impotence, repression, rage, unfathomable depth or unknowable superficiality.

This is all by way of speculating, albeit rather extremely, on what the opposite of Expressionism might be. In its own day, the movement was tempered by the Neue Sachlichkeit, whose artists enforced naturalism and restraint over aggression and subjectivity; they commended the contemporary subject over an imagined mythic one. For painters and sculptors, what the language seemed to call for was photography without a camera. At least, this is one way of seeing how contemporary artists have referenced it. In the wake of Ground Zero cultural operations attempting to rebuild national style from scratch, Gerhard Richter says that as a young artist in Post-war Germany, he found a personal licence to paint when he saw the work of Jackson Pollock in the 1958 Documenta exhibition. He took what he learned from Pollock to his own extreme. Today Richter's ersatz abstract paintings, lush and mechanically void of all conventional "expression," appear as hybrids of Abstract Expressionism and Neue Sachlichkeit; the photo-based paintings, simultaneously sharply blurred and softly realistic, match New Objectivity with Pop. In both cases, the emotional tenor of the work is "expressionless," deliberately cool no matter how potentially incendiary (the terrorist Baader-Meinhof Group), inspiringly elemental (pounds of paint in every color imaginable), or stupifyingly banal (a flower) its subject matter. It's a very stressful situation that can turn a picture of a record-player into a land mine of expectations.

Balkenhol is one of a generation of German artists — Fritsch, Ruff, Struth, among them — whose work can be broadly regarded as working through the stress that Richter created when he made expressionless-ness into an active form of expression. Photography is the modus operandi, in some form or another, for all of this work. It functions indirectly — imperceptibly embedded in metaphors — in Balkenhol's work, which also has the least political currency compared to the more contemporary-looking, critically engaged work of his peers. Instead, his sculptures have recourse to history, to humanism, to a big picture, to a landscape dotted with statues. A recurrent image is of a man or a woman standing on a globe in a vexing display of good, old-fashioned universality. One of the earliest roots that Balkenhol lays claims to through his sculpture yanks this entire discussion out of present day considerations into the fustiest corridors and galleries of the museum.

### *Private Recourses*

*How much wood would a woodchuck chuck,*
*if a woodchuck could chuck wood?*
*As much wood as a woodchuck could,*
*if a woodchuck would chuck wood.*
(Tongue-twister, American traditional)

Encircling the walls of a gallery is a frieze: men, women (mostly reclining), rams, cows, a man with a ladder, a man blowing a horn. In the center of the room is a group of free-standing sculpture: men with their arms at their sides, staring straight ahead. This is not the Old Kingdom display of funerary art in the Egyptian wing of a museum collection, dating to 2500BC, but an installation at the Kunsthalle Basel by Stephan Balkenhol in 1988. Centuries apart, each is commemorative of contemporary life. Packing tombs for the big trip with carved reliefs, paintings and sculpture, Egyptians entered the afterlife with pictures of everything they would need to carry on as before. (After checking in with Osiris and Isis, animal-headed gods bring you to a little patch of heaven where servants, livestock, family members, construction crews, clothes, and jewelry all await, provided they haven't been stolen from your tomb.) Equipped with Balkenhol's hieratic sculpture and relief, we would travel lighter, but no less prepared.

In Egyptian art, life in death on one side is anchored by death in life on the other. Faces are expressionless, bodies are rigidly posed; everything is set for eternity through representations that stop life dead so that one day, after death, it can all be revitalized. And here occurs another favorite theme of photography. A momentary representation, snapped from life, the photograph renders its subject as though for an instant dead. Beyond that moment time rushes forward, the subject ages, dies, disappears, throughout which time the photograph maintains an image of someone frozen in the stream of life. (During the daguerrian era, when the moment it took to take the picture was a prolonged one, sitters were rendered lifeless by contraptions, tools clamped to the backs of their heads that held them in place.) Greco-roman mummy portraits, painted on panels of wood bound to the wrapped corpse, give startlingly realistic, photographic faces to the dead enlivened by the raised texture of wood grain. (Over time, more and more of the wood now shines through.) Eluding death,

Balkenhol's subjects are always in the prime of life, as are most ancient Egyptians. He's sculpted a few youths (Mr. Everyman's younger selves, for example), but no old people. Only the lumber ages — it splits and cracks, the knots weep resin — on these Dorian Grays. His men and women remain uniformly on the early side of middle-age, keeping birth and death equally at bay, planted solidly in the center of a normal life span, not noticeably invested in the here-after. In the case of the (egregiously punning in English) *Man on a Buoy* in the Thames, they literally stand in the stream of life.

They also stand as monuments to a good life in the here-and-now of capitalist culture, where, to paraphrase Balkenhol, we don't usually see infants or geriatrics. Attractive specimens, Balkenhol's solidly built figures are the *Gemütlich* counterparts in sculpture to Alex Katz's painted society of fashionable party-goers. Both artists mediate exchanges between photography, which flickers suggestively, as though buried alive, in their stubborn studio practices. The flow of mechanical reproduction is arrested in their art through the creation of unique, "authentic" objects. In a pair of untitled painted wood reliefs, done by Balkenhol in 1997, two women in stylish summer shifts (one blue, one with red stripes) are seen from behind. They seem to be walking into the planks upon which they are represented, as though turning into wood, undergoing a temporary transmogrification on the other side of which they might just as casually walk out of the sculpture and turn into a pair of paintings by Alex Katz. Conversely, Katz has been known to leave the scene of the party and paint landscapes, most notably the woods, where the trunks of trees circulate throughout the scene like guests.

Balkenhol says that he is cautious about the amount of narrative he admits to his work, "I either avoid it or seek it out, case by case. I used to attempt to eliminate any narrative aspect whatsoever from my works… (for) one must remain vigilant about what is to be told. Up till now I have evoked little folk-tales, or relations between people and animals." Judging from all the different ways he plays with it, scale is one of Balkenhol's preferred methods for admitting a modicum of story without having to tell too much. An installation view shows one of his giant sculpted heads being looked at by a young woman. The room is full of giant heads. As ever, they are the heads of ordinary men and women; the real woman in the room could easily be a model for one of them. Her presence contributes to the uncanny thought that the body might be dispensable and the head could function on its own. (In another work by Balkenhol, Mr. Everyman is actually holding his head under his arm.) In other times and places, oracles, invested with the power to see into and address the future often took the form of big heads. The power of Balkenhol's silent sculptures, however, seems to be purely one of scale. They dwarf the viewer with their gigantism, but at the same time they are reduced by it. Gulliver was grotesquely dragged down by his own bigness among the Lilliputians, whose diminutive size levelled him to a gigantic, eating and shitting creature, an outcast among petite, civilized men and women. Bigness is a sign of sublime and untameable nature, whose presence is accounted for in the clear wooden skins of Balkenhol's heads. Their stylish haircuts, however, pluck them out of the wilderness and set them down squarely in architecture.

Architecture has provided Balkenhol's sculpture with some of its most memorable occasions. A *Very Big Head* had its day on a pylon of Blackfriars Bridge as part of the 1992 group exhibition, *Doubletake*. Men and women, standing on globes, perched on the roof of a building for the South African Biennial. A pair of acrobats posed, one on top of the other, head-to-head inside of the outdoor courtyard of a Swiss bank; a man stood in a niche on the facade of a building of the Staedelgarten in Frankfurt. All these interventions questioned the public role of monuments, which is to impose on the viewer a reminder of the larger structure of history and events, of the institutions of industry and finance upon which they should consider themselves fortunate to depend. Replacing inflated symbols of public life with sculptures of unassuming citizens, Balkenhol, in his friendly way, takes some of the authority out of the larger architecture, bringing it down to size for Everyman and his everyday concerns.

Elsewhere in his travels, Gulliver is shrunk to diminutive size himself, this time suffering the humiliation of becoming a plaything, a tiny pet for a pair of stupendously giant royals, who set him up in a dollhouse for their surveillance and mirth. Likewise, Balkenhol's miniature men and women make them desirable objects, to have and to hold. And unlike Giacometti's tiniest figures (which like Gulliver, were once kept in a matchbox), they remain small in terms of the mental space they command. It's a modernist homily: the concept that sculpture doesn't need to be big to look big, with bigness taken to be a qualitative sign of goodness. But when Balkenhol makes something small it stays that way, allowing one to experience "smallness" where, in a realm of cultural production that typically goes in for grand gestures, one is not accustomed to finding it. A man is sitting under a toadstool. Another man is sitting on the back of a snail; the snail is relatively big, the man ridiculously small; it's a peaceful arrangement. One studies it like a picture, a photograph, with all the information, writ small, and true enough.

### *Animals*

Putting man and beast together turns out to be one of the main objectives of Balkenhol's art. In fairytales, being shrunk to subhuman, rodent size or transformed into an animal is a common form of punishment or evil enchantment performed by witches or sorcerers. In other indigenous lore, animal attributes (a panther's speed, an owl's sharp sight) are coveted extras for basic bodies. In Balkenhol's pantheon, all kinds of exchanges go on without much comment. There's the aforementioned shrinking, plus a bevy of hybridizations. The Everyman is re-tooled as *Three Hybrids* (1995) with the heads of a cow, a tiger and a bird of prey. A man and a woman face-off in a pair of reliefs secreted inside of a divided tree-trunk, *A Travers l'Arbre* (1995); each stands beside its respective *doppelgÑnger*, a fox-headed female and a buck-headed man. Between the four of them, there's not much room for narrative speculation on creatures so wholly transformed.

It's interesting to compare Balkenhol's animal imagery to that of his peer, Katharina Fritsch. Fritsch, whose work involves issues of mechanical reproduction through casting processes, repetitious imagery and multiple objects, has made important installations featuring rats, poodles and an elephant. The animals, like her figurative representations, are stripped-down iconic forms, as she too wants to attract the widest possible identification through her images. When asked, for example, why the giant rats in *Rattenkînig* (1993) did not have genitals, she responded: "I am concerned with basic ideas, and here I am certainly in the minimal art tradition. A vase is first and foremost an object, not a man or a woman. And with animals I am interested in the ambivalent symbolism in which we reflect our human qualities. Unambiguous membership of a particular sex would reduce this ambivalence, make the mirror smaller. If the viewer makes a distinction between male and female at the first or second glance, that's all right, it's just that I don't lay that down definitely."[15]

Thus, like Balkenhol, Fritsch uses images to strike a basic rapport with the viewer. From this initial point the two bodies of work diverge. Fritsch says that she selects her animal subjects with an "ambivalent symbolism" in mind — rats in the popular imagination

[15] Quoted in Matthias Winzen's, "In Conversation with Katharina Fritsch," *Katharina Fritsch*, exhib. cat., San Francisco, Museum of Modern Art, 1996.

are filthy and frightening — which she both amplifies (through scale or some other form of exaggeration) and confounds through her art and its references. Facing out towards the viewer, the room-sized rats are standing in a circle, at the center of which is a giant ball, created by their tails being all knotted together. The artist cites a phenomenon, first observed in medieval times, of rats found inexplicably bound together in this way as her source for the image. It is both repulsive and fascinating. Indeed, the uncanny is a common experience in her work, which sites itself at the twists in simple narratives and pinpoints the weakest links of understanding, thereby underscoring our fears or confusion.

There is no such psychological content in Balkenhol's work, nor is there any underlying story, subjective goal or conceptual narrative. Only recently has he started to admit movement to his work, which comes in part, one suspects, from his increasing ability to make his material do what he wants, to be more expressive in a conventional sense of the word. (Although in the context of this essay, one sees that the gesture-less pose is as much a gesture as the expression-less figure is expressive.) One might even study how a little gesture goes a long way-a man with his hand in one pocket is less relaxed than a man with one shoulder slouched — but this isn't saying much. Balkenhol says he's leaving it up to the viewer, or in this case, the writer, to inform the work with his or her own observations, which the sculpture generously invites, intelligently entertains and then, at its best, completely rejects, as imperviously as a statue. Having run the gamut from photography to sculpture, from bigness to smallness, from ancient art to German art, from crafts to toys, from Everyman to animals, what one is ultimately left with is that with which Balkenhol began and with which he works, oddly enough, through the figure to deliver. What one is left to contemplate is nothing more, or less, than a block of "living" wood.

*About the Artist*

*1957*

Born in Fritzlar/Hessen.

*1976-82*

Studied at the Hamburg School of Fine Arts

*1983*

Awrarded the Karl-Schmidt-Rottluff Grant.

*1986*

Awarded grant by the city of Hamburg

*1988-89*

Lecturer at the Hamburg School of Fine Arts

*1989*

Awarded the Baden-Württemberg International Prize, and the Bremen Art Prize.

*1990-91*

Lecturer at the Frankfurt School of Fine Arts (Städelschule).

*1991-92*

Lecturer at the Karlsruhe Fine Arts Academy.

*1992*

Professor of sculptureat the Karlsruhe Academy of Fine Art.

Stephan Balkenhol lives and works in Karlsruhe (Germany) and in Meisenthal (France)

## *Solo Exhibitions* (selection)

*1985*

Kunstverein, Bochum

*1987*

Kunstverein, Braunschweig

*1988*

Galerie Löhrl, Mönchengladbach

Kunsthalle, Basel (with Marika Mäkelä and Dennis Hopper)

Galerie Johnen & Schöttle, Cologne

*1988-89*

Portikus, Frankfurt

*1989*

Galerie Rüdiger Schöttle, Munich

Kunsthalle, Nürnberg

Staatliche Kunsthalle, Baden-Baden (with Artur Stoll)

*1991*

Städelgarten, Frankfurt

Kunstverein, Ulm

The Irish Museum of Modern Art, Royal Hospital Kilmainham, Dublin

*1992*

Kunsthalle, Hamburg

Galerie Roger Pailhas, Marseille

Witte de With, Rotterdam

*1994*

Kunstverein, Wolfsburg

Nationalgalerie, Berlin (with Carsten Nikolai)

Musée de Rochechouart/Musée de Dôle/FRAC Haute Normandie, Sotteville-les-Rouen

*1995*

Hirshhorn Museum, Washington D.C.

*1996*

Musée des Beaux-Arts, Montréal

Galerie Rüdiger Schöttle, Cologne/Galerie Bernd Klüser, Münich

C.E.A.A.C. Strasbourg

Galerie Mai 36, Zürich

Regen Projects, Los Angeles

*1997*

Galerie Löhrl, Mönchengladbach

Barbara Gladstone Gallery, New York

Galerie Johnen & Schöttle, Cologne

## *Group Exhibitions* (selection)

*1986*

« Jenisch Park », sculpture exhibition, Hamburg.

*1987*

« Skulptur Projekte », Westfallian Museum, Munster..

*1988*

« The Binationale German Art of the Late 80's / American Art of the Late 80's », Kunsthalle/Kunstverein/Kunstsammlung Nordrhein-Westfalen, Düsseldorf ; Museum of Fine Art, Boston/Houston/-Baltimore.

*1989*

« Prospekt '89' », Kunstverein and Schirn Kunsthalle, Frankfurt.

*1990*

« Possible Worlds, Sculpture from Europe », Serpentine Gallery/ICA, London.

***1992***

« Double Take ; Collective Memory and Current Act », Hayward Gallery, London

« Expo'92 », Seville

« Post Human », FAE Musée d'Art Contemporain, Lucern

« Qui, Quoi, Où ? Un regard sur l'art en Allemagne en 1992 », ARC, Paris

***1993***

« Post Human », Deichtorhallen, Hamburg

***1994***

« Still-Life », Barbara Gladstone Gallery, New York

***1995***

« Zeichen und Wunder », Kunsthaus Zürich

« Africus », Biennale de Johannesburg

« 1995 Carnegie International », Pittsburgh

***1996***

« Les contes de fées se terminent bien », FRAC Haute-Normandie, Rouen

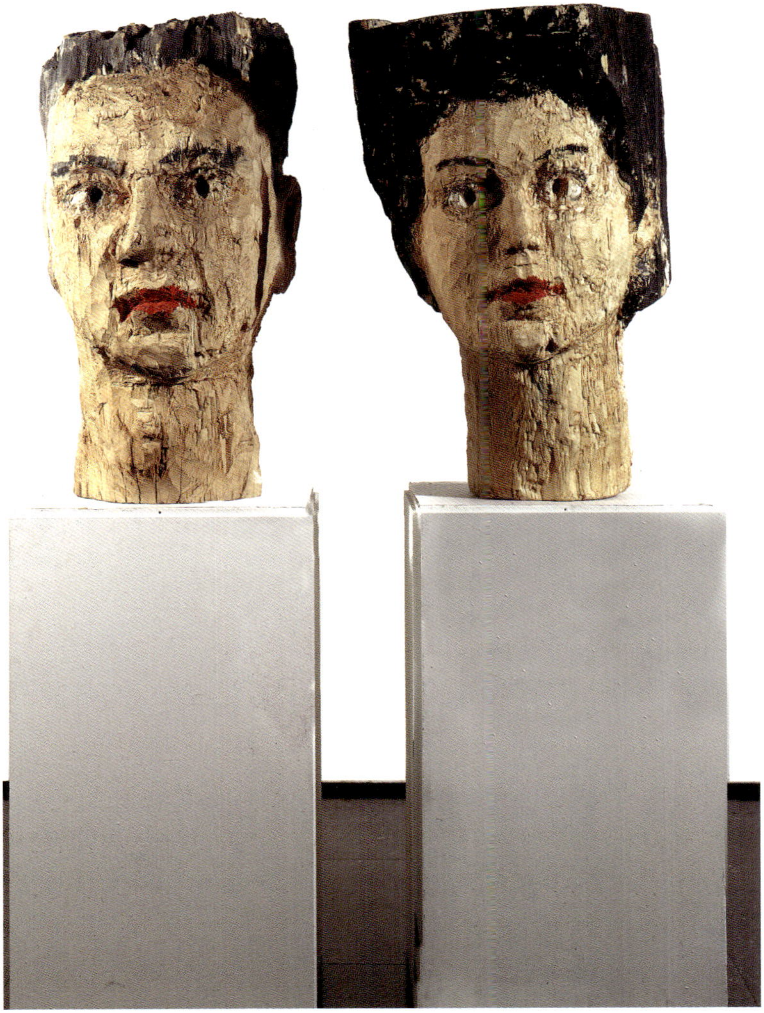

◄ 1

2 ►

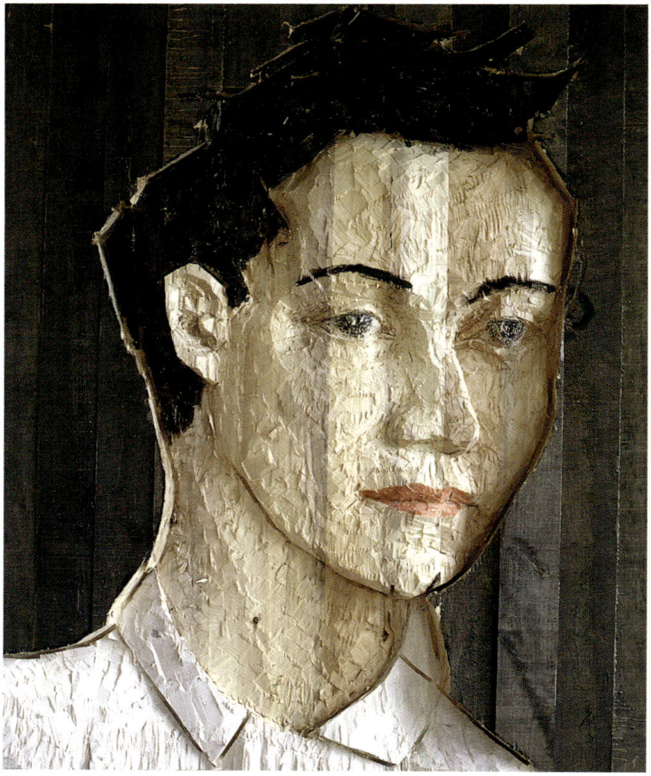

◀ 3

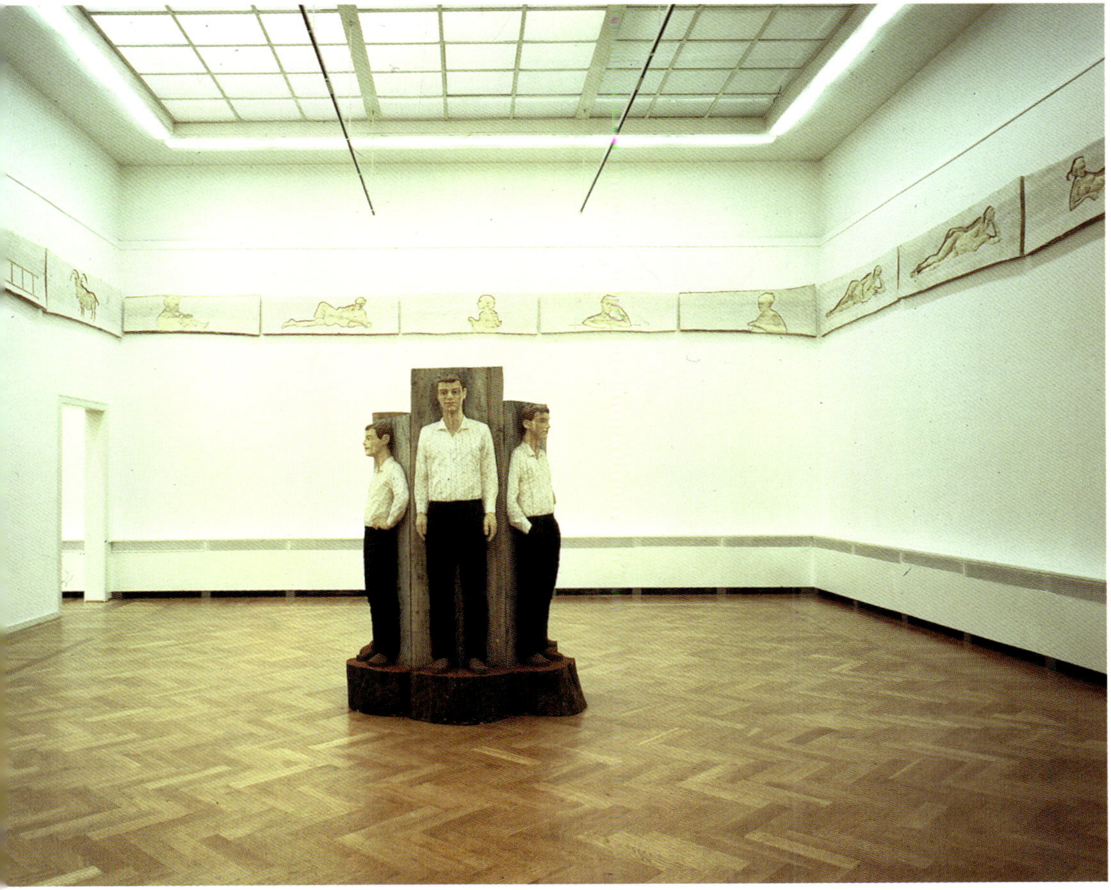

4 ▶

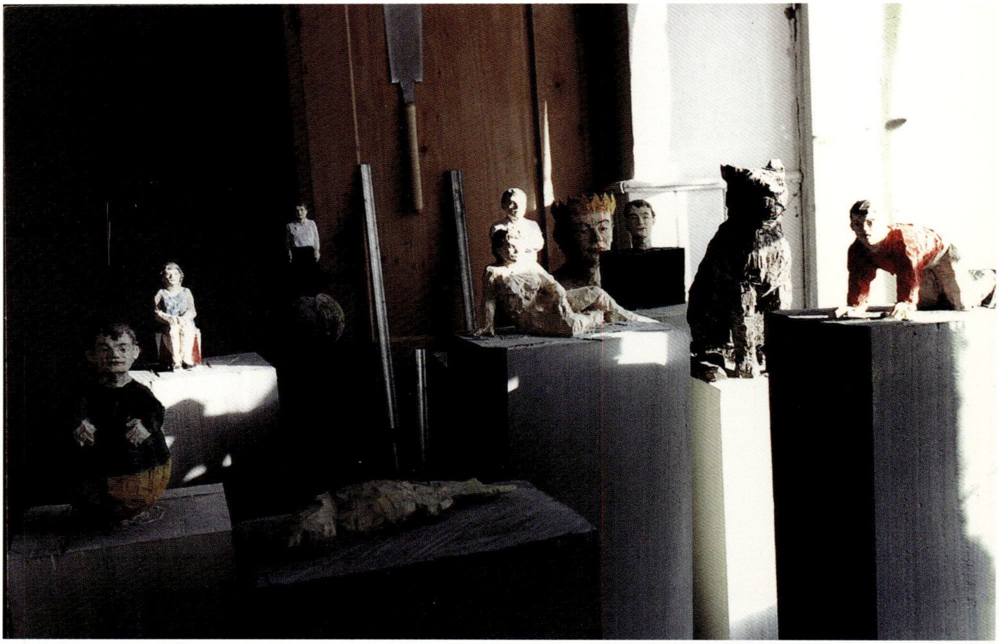

◀ 5

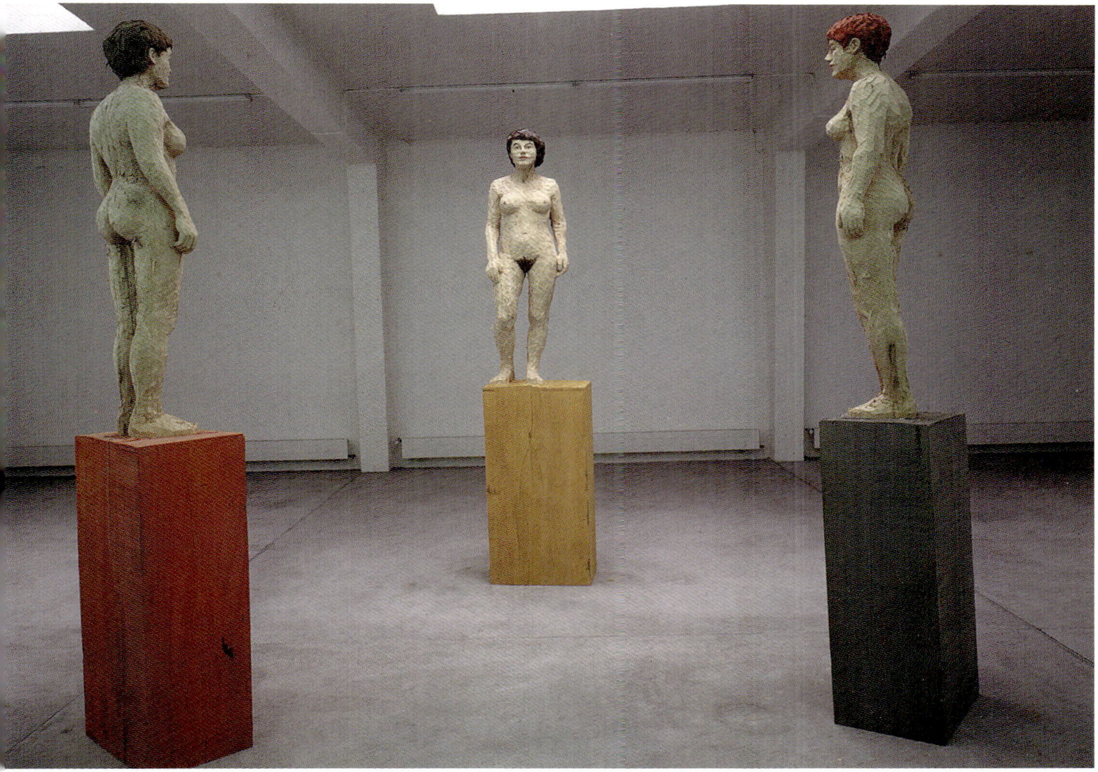

6 ▶

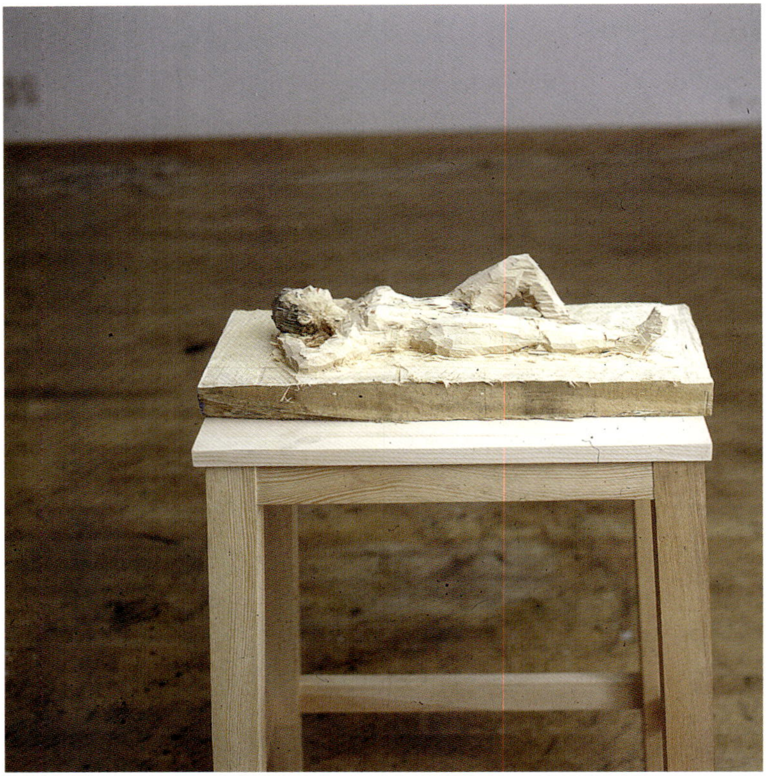

◀ 7

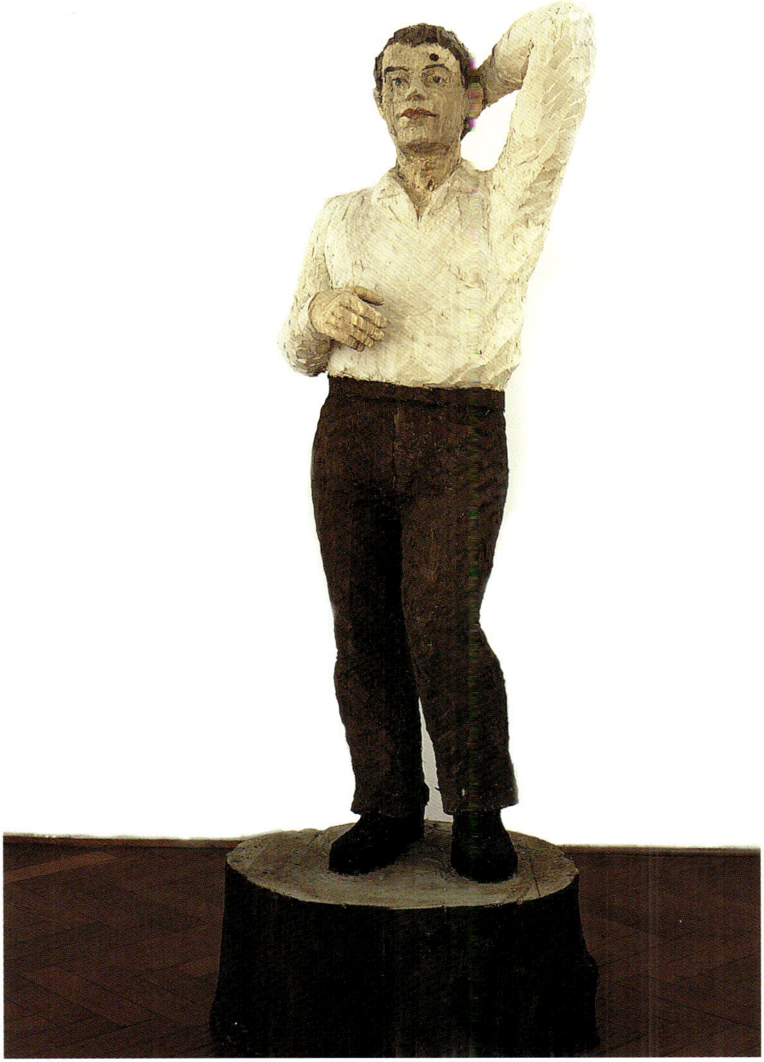

8 ▶

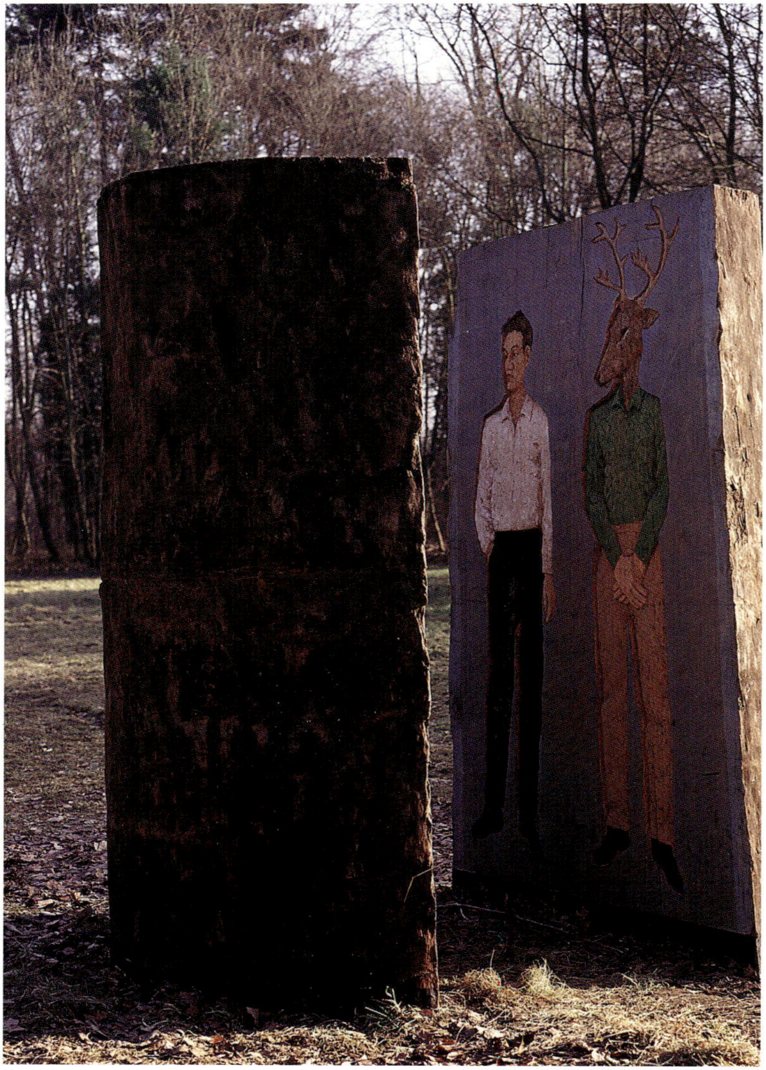

◀ 9

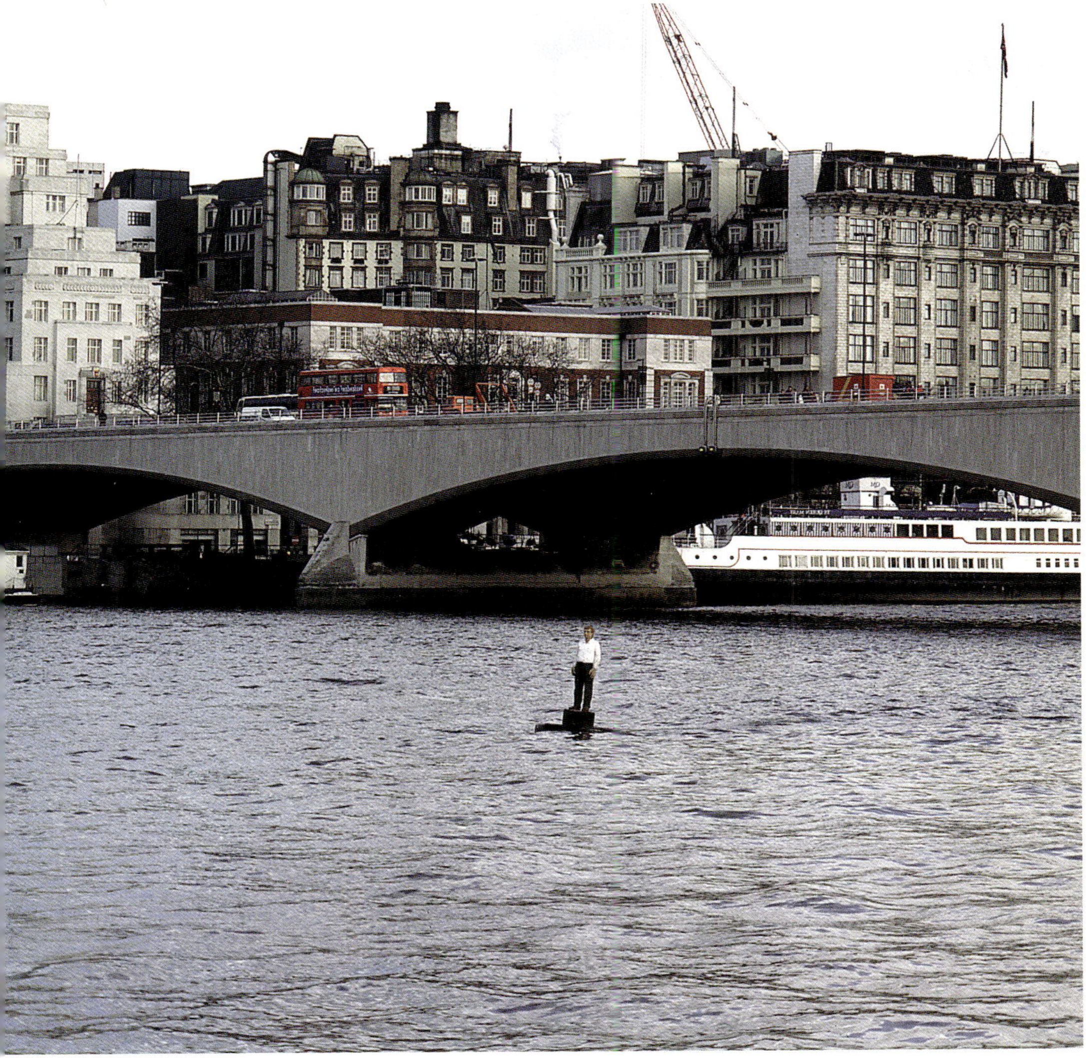

10 ▶

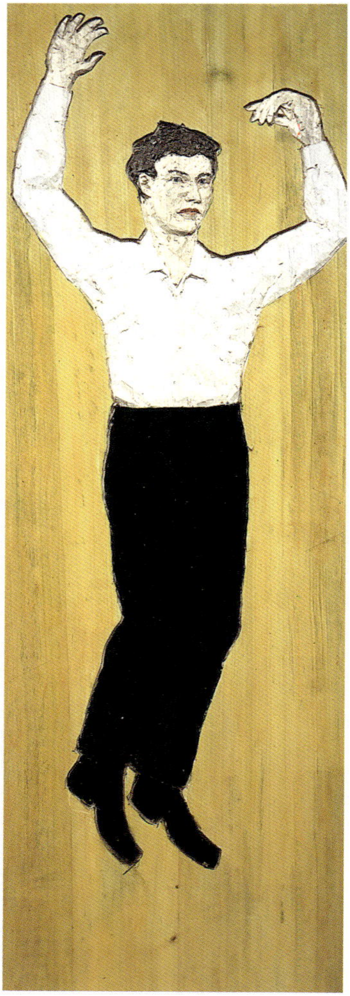

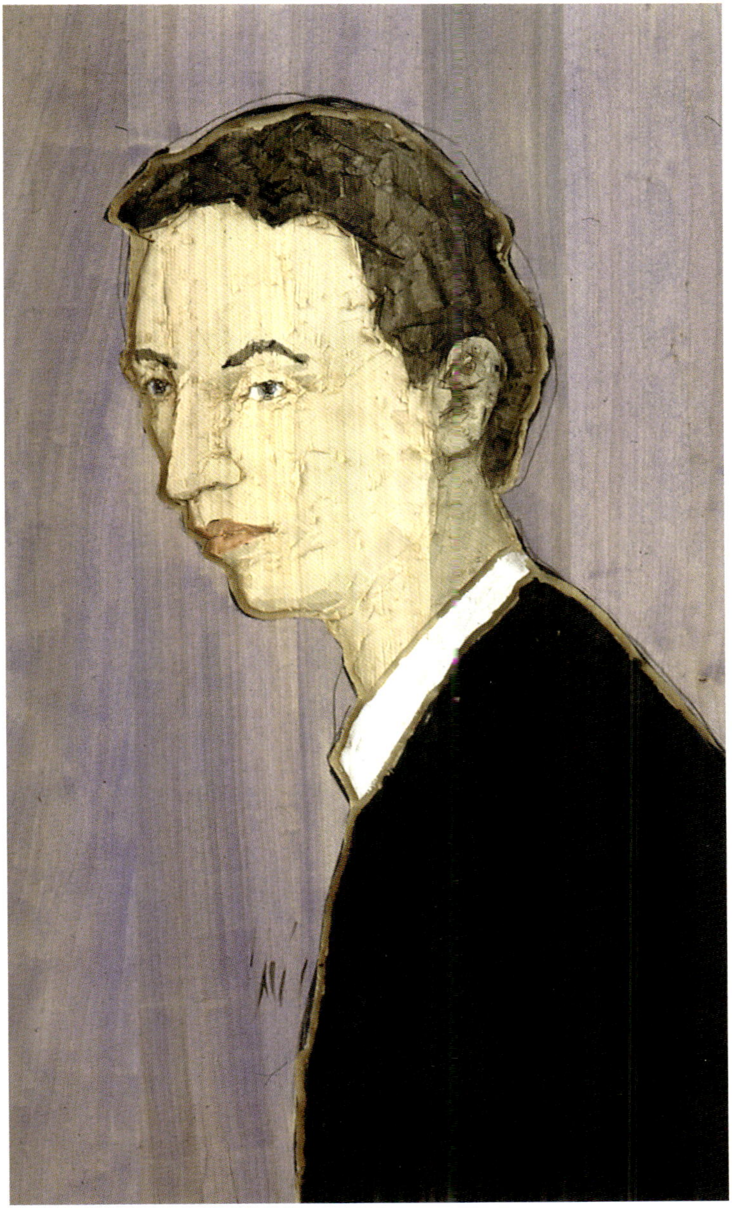

◄ 11

12 ▶

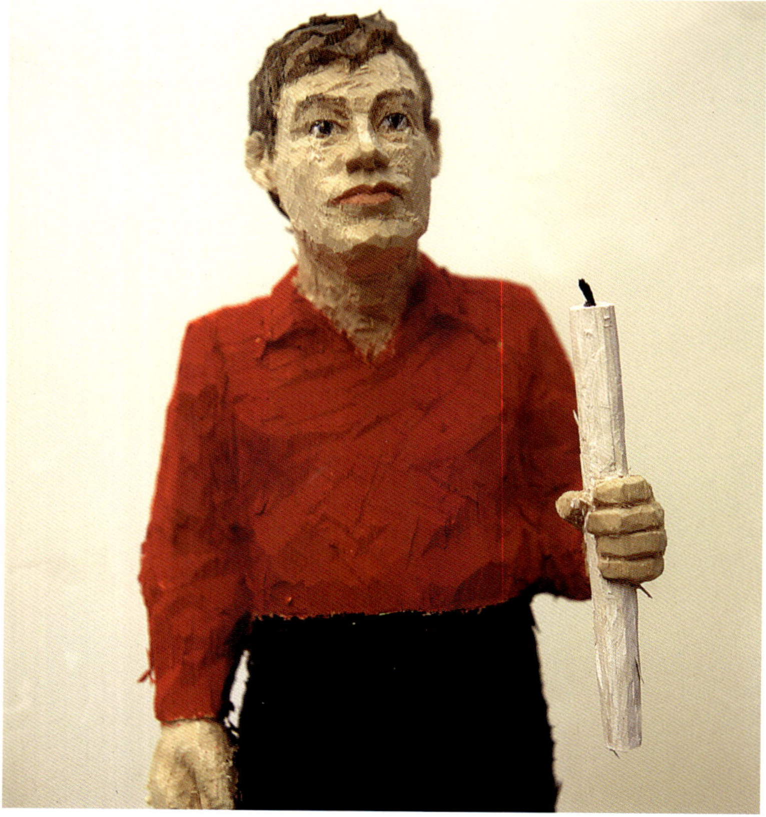

◀ 13 ◀ 14

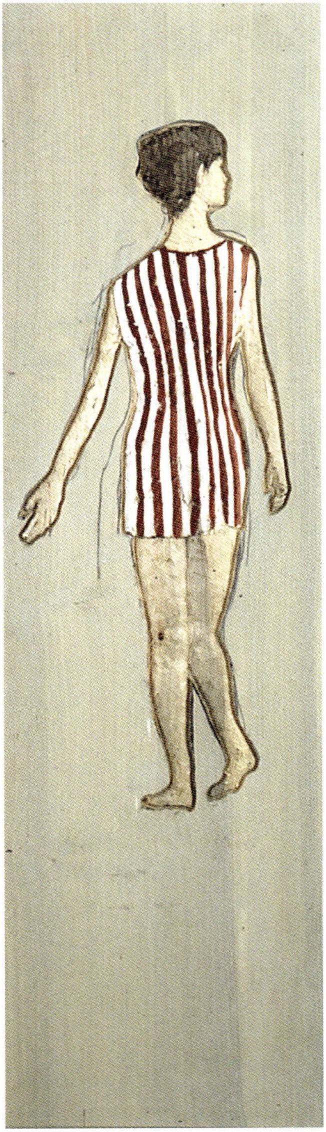

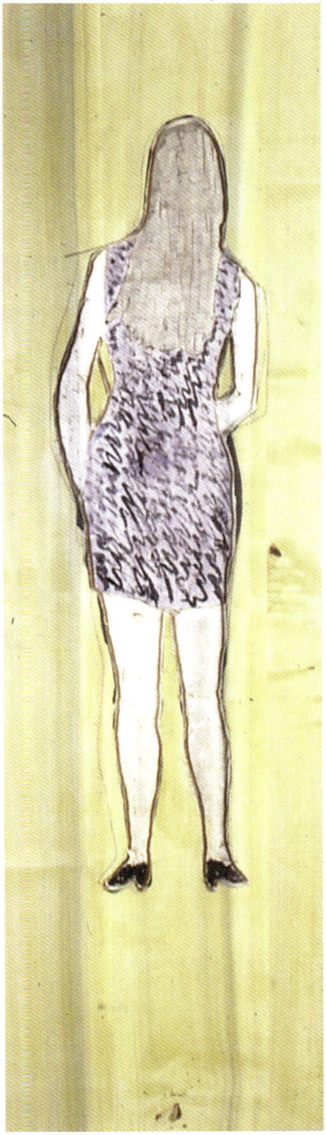

15 ▶

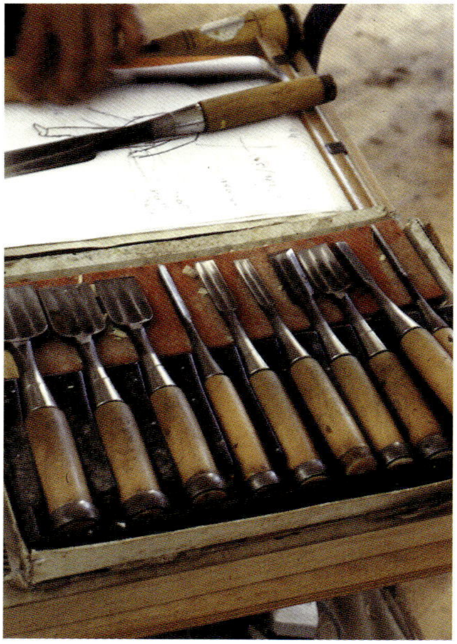

◀ 16

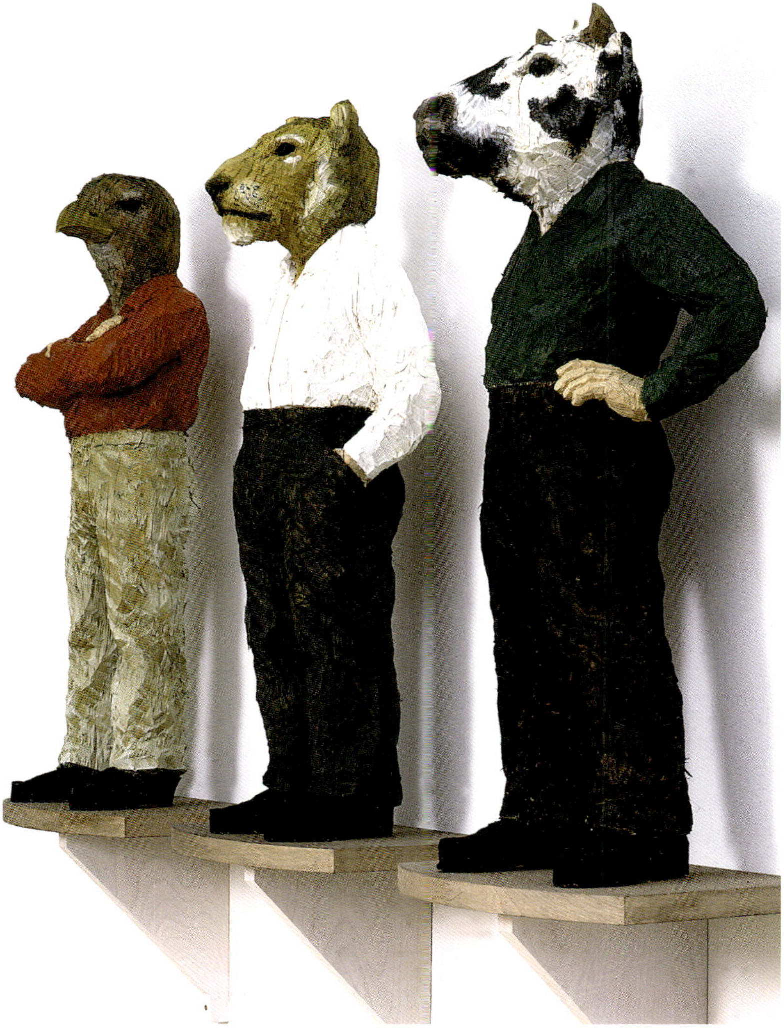

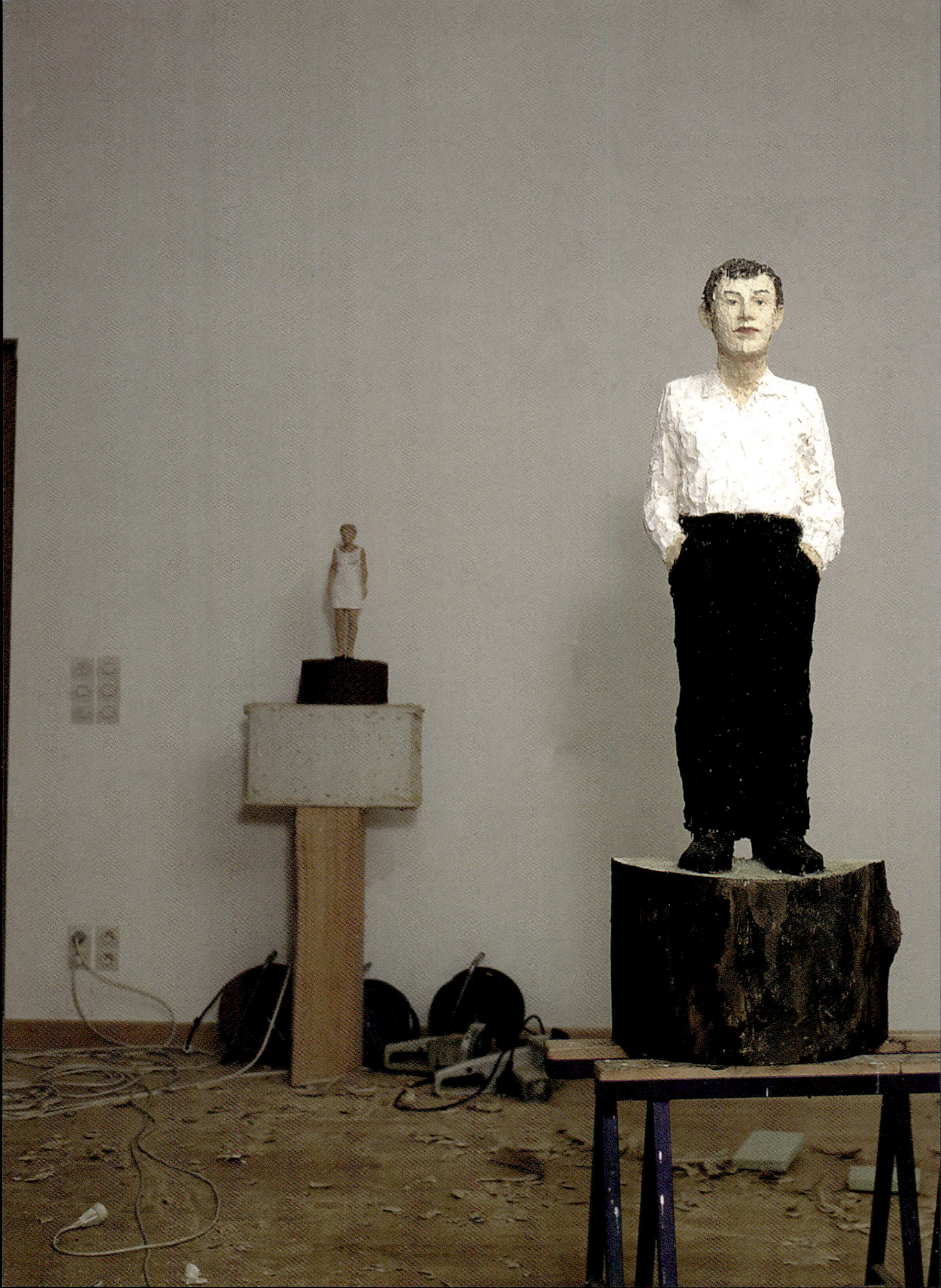

◀◀17

◀ 18

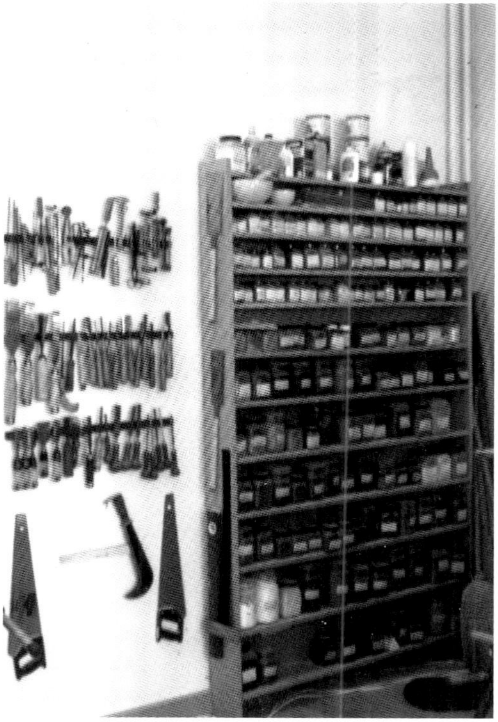

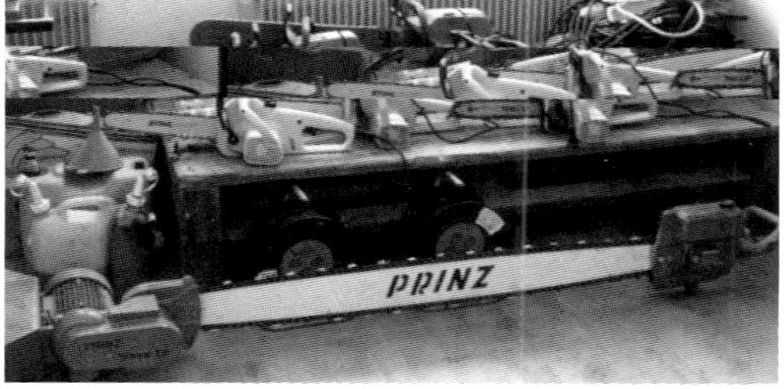


◀ 19

*Index Photos*

1: *Untitled* (male head), 1982
96,5x66cm
*Untitled* (female head),1982
95x66cm
Poplar wood, painted.
Ph: Anne Gold,
Courtesy Lüdwig Forum für Internationale Kunst.

2: *Large Relief (Man's Head)* , 1989
Poplar wood, painted, 140x150x10cm

3: *Hexagon and Frieze,* 1988
*Hexagon,* Copperbeech wood, painted
2x(200x62x45cm), 2x(210x62x45cm), 2x(235x62x45cm)
*Frieze* (twenty-sided)
Poplar wood, painted
[10 x(215x75x4cm), 10x(185x75x4cm)]
Courtesy Galerie Löhrl

4: *Group of ten small sculptures*, 1992
Wawa wood, paint, 120-160cm

5: *Three Large Female Nudes,* 1993
Wawa wood, painted, ca. 300 cm.
Courtesy Galerie Johnen & Schöttle, Cologne

6: *Woman lying down*, 1997
Wawa wood, 60x30x15cm.

7: *Large Classical Man*, 1996
Poplar wood, painted, 250x86x77cm
Ph: Mario Gastinger,
Courtesy Galerie Bernd Klüser

8: *Through the Tree*, 1996
Bubinga wood carved and painted, diametre 240cm/220cm
Parc de Sculpture Contemporaine de Pourtalés, Strasbourg.

9: *Standing Figure on a Buoy*, (Thames River) 1992
Oak, metal, 250x50x40cm
Artist's collection

10: *Large Relief Plate* (yellow), 1996
Poplar wood, painted, 283x102,5x3,5cm
Ph: Mario Gastinger
Courtesy Galerie Bernd Klüser

11: *Untitled* (Relief, Man in Black), 1997
Poplar wood, acrylic color, 100x60x3cm
Ph : David Regen
Courtesy Barbara Gladstone

12: *Man with a Candle*, 1997
Wawa wood, paint, 157cm

13: *Untitled* (Relief, Woman in Stripes), 1997
Poplar wood, acrylic color, 200x60x3cm
Photo: David Regen
Courtesy Barbara Gladstone

14: *Untitled* (Relief, Woman in Blue), 1997
Poplar wood, acrylic color, 200x60x3cm
Photo: David Regen
Courtesy Barbara Gladstone

15: In the Artist's Studio, 1997
Ph: Hervé Vanel

16: *Hybrids*, 1995.
Cedar, 121,3x 50,2x34,3cm
Ph: Larry Lame
Courtesy Barbara Gladstone Gallery

17: The Artist's Studio, 1996

18/19: In the Artist's Studio, 1997
Ph: Hervé Vanel

## *Bibliography* (selection)

Dietrich Helms, *Impulse* 1, Galerie Löhrl, Mönchengladbach, 1983

Ulrich Rückriem, *Stephan Balkenhol - Skulpturen*, Austellungshallen Mathildenhöhe, Darmstadt, 1985.

Bernd Ernsting, *Jenisch-Park Skulptur*, Hambour, 1986.

Wilhelm Bojescul, Ludger Gerdes, *Stephan Balkenhol, Skulpturen und Zeichnungen*, Kunstverein, Braunschweig, 1987.

Günther Gercken, *Neue Kunst in Hamburg*, Hambourg, 1987.
Ammann Jean-Christophe, Jeff Wall, *Stephan Balkenhol*, Kunsthalle Bâle, 1988.

Stephan Balkenhol, *Zeichnungen 1990 und Entwürfe für skulpturen*, Deweer Art Gallery, Otegem., 1990.

Lynne Cooke, Bice Curiger and Greg Hilty, *Doubletake, Collective Memory and Current Art*, Hayward Gallery, Londres, 1992.

Stephan Balkenhol, James Lingwood, Jeff Wall; interview de Ulrich Rückriem et Thomas Schütte, *Stephan Balkenhol, über Menschen und Skulpturen*, Witte de With Center for Contemporary Art, Ed. Crantz, Stuttgart, 1992.

Britta Schmitz, *Stephan Balkenhol: Skulpturen*, Neue Nationalgalerie, Berlin, 1994.

Susanne Pfleger, Klaus Hoffmann, Stephan Balkenhol, *Skulpturen und Zeichnungen,* Mönchengladbach, 1994.

Alexandra Midal (interview), Frédéric Migayrou, *Stephan Balkenhol*, Musée Départemental d'Art Contemporain, Rochechouart,1994.

Klaus Gallwitz, *Africus: Johannesburg Biennale 95*, Johannesbourg.

James T. Demetrion, Neal Benezra, *Stephan Balkenhol Sculptures and Drawings*, Hirshhorn Museum, Washington, 1995.

*Also available from Dis Voir*

*PLASTIC ARTS*

François Dagognet
*In Favour of Today's Art*

Jean-Yves Bosseur
*Sound and the Visual Arts*

Thierry de Duve
*Clement Greenberg between the lines*

Alain Charre, Marie-Paule MacDonald, Marc Perelman
*Dan Graham*

Gertrud Koch, Luc Lang, Jean-Philippe Antoine
*Gerhard Richter*

Christine Savinel, Jacques Roubaud, Bernard Noël
*Roman Opalka*

Christine Macel, Marc Perelman, Jacinto Lageira
*Jean-Marc Bustamante*

Jeff Wall, Ludger Gerdes, Hervé Vanel, Ingrid Schaffner
*Stephan Balkenhol*

*LITERATURE / FINE ART / CINEMA*

Raúl Ruiz

*Poetics of Cinema*
*The Book of Disappearances & The Book of Tractations*
*A la Poursuite de l'Ile au Trésor*

Peter Greenaway

*The Falls*
*Rosa*
*Fear of Drowning by Numbers*
*Papers - (Paintings, Collages and Drawings)*
*The Cook, the Thief, his Wife and her Lover*
*The Baby of Mâcon*
*The Pillow Book*

Manoel de Oliveira

*Les Cannibales*

*CINEMA*

Jean-Marc Lalanne, Ackbar Abbas, David Martinez, Jimmy Ngai

*Wong Kar-wai*

Paul Virilio, Carole Desbarats, Jacinto Lageira, Danièle Rivière

*Atom Egoyan*

Michael Nyman, Daniel Caux, Michel Field, Florence de Mèredieu, Philippe Pilard

*Peter Greenaway*

Christine Buci-Glucksmann, Fabrice Revault d'Allonnes

*Raúl Ruiz*

Yann Lardeau, Jacques Parsi, Philippe Tancelin

*Manoel de Oliveira*

*CHOREOGRAPHY*

Paul Virilio, René Thom, Laurence Louppe, Jean-Noël Laurenti, Valérie Preston-Dunlop

*Traces of Dance - Drawings and Notations of Choreographers*

*ARCHITECTURE*

Christian de Portzamparc

*Genealogy of forms*

*DESIGN*

Raymond Guidot, Olivier Boissière

*Ron Arad*

François Burkhardt, Cristina Morozzi

*Andrea Branzi*

ÉDITIONS DIS VOIR : 3, RUE BEAUTREILLIS - F-75004 PARIS

PHONE (33 - 1) 48 87 07 09 - FAX (33 - 1) 48 87 07 14